MW00779911

Lead wIth Prayer

LEAD wITH PRAYER

THE SPIRITUAL HABITS OF
WORLD-CHANGING LEADERS

Ryan Skoog,
Peter Greer, and
Cameron Doolittle
with Jill Heisey

Foreword by John Mark Comer

NASHVILLE   NEW YORK

Jacket design by Gabriella Wikidal
Jacket copyright © 2024 by Hachette Book Group, Inc.

FaithWords
Hachette Book Group
1290 Avenue of the Americas, New York, NY 10104
faithwords.com
twitter.com/faithwords

First Edition: January 2024

FaithWords is a division of Hachette Book Group, Inc. The FaithWords name and logo are trademarks of Hachette Book Group, Inc.

The publisher is not responsible for websites (or their content) that are not owned by the publisher.

The Hachette Speakers Bureau provides a wide range of authors for speaking events. To find out more, go to hachettespeakersbureau.com or email HachetteSpeakers@hbgusa.com.

FaithWords books may be purchased in bulk for business, educational, or promotional use. For information, please contact your local bookseller or the Hachette Book Group Special Markets Department at special.markets@hbgusa.com.

Unless otherwise indicated, Scripture quotations are taken from THE HOLY BIBLE, NEW INTERNATIONAL VERSION®, NIV® Copyright © 1973, 1978, 1984, 2011 by Biblica, Inc.® Used by permission. All rights reserved worldwide.

Additional Scripture information is on page 224.

Library of Congress Cataloging-in-Publication Data

Names: Skoog, Ryan, author. | Greer, Peter, 1975- author. | Doolittle, Cameron, author. | Heisey, Jill, author.
Title: Lead with prayer : the spiritual habits of world-changing leaders / Ryan Skoog, Peter Greer, and Cameron Doolittle, with Jill Heisey.
Description: First edition. | Nashville : FaithWords, 2024.
Identifiers: LCCN 2023031126 | ISBN 9781546005629 (hardcover) | ISBN 9781546005643 (ebook)
Subjects: LCSH: Leadership—Religious aspects. | Prayer.
Classification: LCC BL325.L4 S56 2024 | DDC 206/.1—dc23/eng/20230811
LC record available at https://lccn.loc.gov/2023031126

ISBNs: 9781546005629 (hardcover), 9781546005643 (ebook)

Printed in the United States of America

LSC-C

Printing 1, 2023

CONTENTS

PART I
HOW LEADERS PRIORITIZE PRAYER

PART II
HOW LEADERS GROW IN THEIR PRAYER LIFE

PART III
HOW LEADERS MULTIPLY PRAYER WITHIN THEIR ORGANIZATIONS

The shepherds are senseless
    and do not inquire of the Lord;
so they do not prosper
    and all their flock is scattered.
               —Jeremiah 10:21

FOREWORD

There's a saying from the business world I love: "Leaders eat last." Meaning, leaders put others ahead of themselves, a principle we Christians call "servant leadership." Nowhere do we see this type of leadership more clearly than in Jesus Himself.

Yet there's another key leadership principle we see throughout Jesus' life example, that of prayer. Jesus' ministry *began* with forty days in the wilderness devoted to prayer; in story after story, we see Him return to this prayerful place, and then reemerge to follow His Father's direction. We could articulate it as "Leaders pray *first*."

I think of Luke's biographical line: "Jesus often withdrew to lonely places and prayed" (Luke 5:16). The original Greek can also be translated Jesus "frequently withdrew...and prayed" (NET) or He "often slipped away...so he could pray" (NCV) or "as often as possible Jesus withdrew to out-of-the-way places for prayer" (MSG).

Jesus was no hermit; He was an active, busy leader, yet He intentionally carved out vast swaths of time to pray. When I hear leaders say "I'm too busy to pray like that," or "I just don't have the time to go away," I grieve. Why do we think we could live and lead without what Jesus Himself considered essential?

It's no surprise that Jesus' apprentices, captivated by their rabbi's beautiful life, once said to Him, "Teach us to pray." It seems that after watching their Lord "behind the scenes," they had come to the conclusion that Jesus' extraordinary *outer* life of power was the result of an even *more* extraordinary *inner* life of prayer. That in His frequent disappearances into the quiet to pray, Jesus was drawing from a deep well of wisdom, direction, power, and courage in God. And they wanted access to that same water.

This ancient well of life in God is still available for any who apprentice under Jesus.

In *Lead with Prayer*, Ryan, Cameron, and Peter have given us a reliable pathway to that ancient well. Their survey of the private prayer lives of well-respected leaders across the boundaries of the church, nonprofit, and business worlds is—in and of itself—worth the read. But their summary and synthesis of these great ones of the Way is the rarefied gift.

You will walk away, as I did, convicted, inspired, instructed, and encouraged—to pray.

But remember: Prayer isn't an *idea*; it's a *practice*. That was one of my favorite things about this book: each chapter ends with a spiritual exercise to turn the vision of becoming a praying leader into a *reality*, to go from information and inspiration to *formation*.

After all, Jesus Himself said, "whoever *practices* and teaches" His Way "will be called great in the kingdom of heaven" (Matthew 5:19, emphasis added).

Leaders pray first.

John Mark Comer
Founder of Practicing the Way

THE LEADERS IN THIS BOOK

In writing this book, we had the immense privilege of learning from many whom we admire for their prayerful leadership. We're grateful to those who generously shared their time, anecdotes, and wisdom with us in first-person interviews, as was the case with most contemporary leaders on this list. In a few cases, and certainly with respect to historical figures, we relied on public sources. Below is a list of these leaders, along with the chapters in which they're discussed.

Christine Baingana (chapter 4)
Mark Batterson (chapter 11 and conclusion)
Richard Beaumont (chapter 10)
Terry Boynton (chapter 2)
Brother Andrew (chapter 7)
Brother Lawrence (chapter 3)
Christine Caine (chapter 12)
Regi Campbell (chapter 12)
Francis Chan (chapter 1)
John Mark Comer (chapter 2)
David Denmark (case study)
Joni Eareckson Tada (chapter 5)
Mary Elizabeth Ellett (chapter 14)
Ganesh (chapter 5)
David Green (chapter 3)
Gary Haugen (chapter 14)
Ignatius of Loyola (chapter 8)
Jean (chapter 8)
Patrick Johnson (chapter 9)

Rob Ketterling (chapter 8)
John Kim (chapter 1)
Peter Kubasek (chapter 13)
Terry Looper (chapters 5 and 7)
Tim Mackie (chapters 6 and 10)
André Mann (chapter 12)
Jay Martin (chapter 14)
Alexander McLean (chapter 6)
Don Millican (chapter 4)
Judah Mooney (chapter 13)
Mother Teresa (chapter 1)
Florence Muindi (chapter 11)
George Müller (chapter 7)
Ibrahim Omondi (chapter 1)
John Ortberg (chapter 4)
Pavel (chapter 9)
Todd Peterson (chapter 11)
John Piper (chapter 6)
Jamie Rasmussen (chapter 8)
Rosebell (introduction and chapter 1)
Hala Saad (chapter 10)
Steve Shackelford (chapter 11)
Shalom (chapters 2, 13, and 14)
Priscilla Shirer (chapter 7)
David Sykora (chapter 12)
Aila Tasse (chapter 7)
Jon Tyson (chapter 14)
Evelyn Underhill (chapter 10)
Justin Whitmel Earley (chapter 4)
Dallas Willard (chapters 3, 9, and 10)
David Wills (chapter 12)
Japhet Yanmekaa (chapters 6 and 9)
Zehra (chapter 3)
Mark Zhou (chapter 3)
Nikolaus Ludwig von Zinzendorf (chapter 14)

NOTE ON ADDITIONAL TOOLS AND RESOURCES

More than a book that you are about to read, we want *Lead with Prayer* to be highly practical. It's our privilege to provide supplementary tools and resources to help you develop your prayer life and a culture of prayer in your organization.

On our website, www.leadwithprayer.com, you'll find:

- A free deck of prayer cards to develop your prayer life and teach those you lead how to pray
- A personal prayer assessment tool
- An organizational prayer assessment tool
- Suggestions for further reading to deepen your prayer life
- Case studies of prayerful organizations
- Bonus interview content
- A link for making bulk purchases of *Lead with Prayer* for your team or network .

In addition, we realized that organizations have systems for (almost) everything that matters: accounting systems for managing money, HR systems for serving employees, messaging systems for communication. *But most of us have no system for the most important process in our ministry: the prayer process.*

We have partnered with Echo Prayer to create **a prayer request distribution app**, as well as other tools that will help leaders implement prayer systems. We believe these tools provide "handles" to help leaders move from just talking about prayer to equipping organizations and teams to more fully practice prayer.

Of course, prayer itself is a relationship, not a piece of software or a process! But we learned from praying leaders that a system can stream-line gathering, filtering, and sharing prayer points across a team. And so we've created what we believe are simple and structured ways to invest in prayer. Learn more on our website.

A portion of the proceeds from this book will fund global prayer movements.

LEADERS HAVE A PRAYER PROBLEM

Don't let the wise boast in their wisdom, or the powerful boast in their power, or the rich boast in their riches. But those who wish to boast should boast in this alone: that they truly know me.

—Jeremiah 9:23–24 NLT

Oh no! I've lost Billy Graham!"

The security guard panicked. He had one job to do: watch the backstage of the auditorium to make sure Billy Graham was safe. He had walked out the door for a moment to check the alleyway, then returned back inside—and in that brief moment, he lost the world's most famous preacher.

Searching backstage, he heard a desperate voice crying out from the catwalk, and when he climbed to the top, he found Billy Graham on his face, pleading in prayer, "God, I cannot do this without You! God, I need Your strength and power to speak today."[1]

That day Billy Graham was preparing to address a midsize group of leaders for only fifteen minutes.

If anyone could deliver a fifteen-minute talk in his own strength or gravitas, it would have been Billy Graham, an incredibly talented orator who literally spoke to millions of people, and met and talked with the most powerful leaders on earth.

But instead, Billy Graham prayed as if the exact opposite were true. He fell on his face, crying out desperately to God. Despite his experience, qualifications, and position as a global leader, Billy Graham lived with a heightened awareness of his reliance on God: an awareness evidenced in his prayer life.

Billy Graham seemed to take Jesus at His word when He said, "Apart from me you can do nothing" (John 15:5). But based on recent studies, it's clear that few lead out of a similar conviction today. Collectively we've lost the essence of Billy Graham: his prayerful dependence on God to sustain his leadership.

The Dispiriting Studies on Prayer

Personally and anecdotally we know that Christian leaders often lead out of our own strength, dedicating significant time to research, strategy, and discussion before rounding out our efforts with a quick prayer for God to bless our plans.

Studies of Christian leaders have drawn the same conclusion: By and large, they report lackluster prayer lives. One study, for example, showed that only 16 percent of pastors are very satisfied with their prayer lives.[2] Another study revealed that 72 percent of pastors identify "consistency in personal prayer" as one of the greatest needs they must address.[3] When it comes to prayer, the gap between where we are and where we want to be is vast.

Expanding beyond pastors, a large foundation in the United States commissioned a top-tier research firm to investigate prayer practices within Christian organizations. They invested six figures in both quantitative and qualitative research to understand how these organizations prayed and what the impact of prayer was on their mission and staff.

Researchers compiled a list of 200 Christian organizations that publicly touted a culture of prayer. This select group was meant to represent the vanguard of organizational prayer, and everyone involved in the study eagerly awaited the results to see what they could learn from these exemplars. The report captured some sad realities facing the Church and parachurch organizations. Specifically, that intentional corporate prayer is the exception and not the norm in Christian organizations.[4]

If this is the disappointing reality about prayer among pastors and leading organizations, how much bleaker is the landscape for everyone else? And if Christian leaders aren't praying, what is the impact on the environments and teams they lead?

Crisis Level

This is no small issue, because there are indeed consequences when leaders do not pray. As the late pastor Tim Keller warned, prayerlessness is *detrimental* for a Christian, but it's *death* for a Christian leader.[5] "Prayerlessness will kill you. It won't just hurt you; it'll kill you," he told a group of Christian leaders. He went on, "The more successful your church [or organization, or small group] is, the more likely you're going to feel too busy for [prayer]. And that's deadly...It is utterly deadly."[6]

And we see Keller's warning playing out as Christian leaders all around us publicly stumble and fall or succumb to burnout and resign their influential roles.

We also see it clearly in Scripture. We know the stories of the great leaders of the Bible, and that many of them stumbled. When leadership scholar J. Robert Clinton studied biblical leaders, he found that only 30 percent "finished well." He believes even fewer are finishing well today, and the connection to prayer is causal and clear: "In latter ministry, the tendency is to rely on competency, one's ability to do things, rather than primarily on God."[7] For competent leaders, Clinton suggests, their "very strength becomes a weakness."[8]

Neglecting prayer is not just disastrous for leaders; it is disastrous for organizations, too. Just as plants eventually wilt without water, an organization that is not refreshed and nourished by prayer will grow lifeless and lose its vitality. Divisions grow. Staff members become disgruntled and disengaged. Organizations increase in busyness but decrease in effectiveness. An organization that neglects prayer is actively decaying.

The Spark

Over the years, we (Ryan, Peter, and Cameron) have often discussed the personal and organizational ramifications of neglecting our prayer lives. Despite our growing awareness of the dangers, a single Bible verse brought the conviction that launched this book.

One day during my normal time of Bible reading, I (Ryan) read the words of 1 Samuel 12:23, in which the prophet and leader Samuel says to the people of Israel, "Far be it from me that I should sin against the Lord by failing to pray for you." I put down my Bible, stood up, and began pacing. Samuel's words convicted me personally as a business and nonprofit leader, and they also seemed to issue a broader challenge to Christian leaders who have made prayer a last resort rather than a first priority. Questions flooded my mind: *Does God consider leaders' failure to pray a sin against Him? Does He hold leaders to a higher standard when it comes to prayer?*

There are thousands of leaders talking about leadership, but what are the prayer lives that fuel their leadership?

And if prayer is the foundation of their lives as leaders, why don't we hear more about it?

I decided to explore the prayer lives of leaders, and I invited Cameron and Peter into this exploration as fellow leaders of global nonprofits. We began by just asking each other, *What should a leader's prayer life look like?* At first, the discussion was just for our own benefit and that of the organizations we lead: VENTURE, Practicing the Way, and HOPE International, respectively. But over time our discussion expanded to research, and we've spent the last three years investigating how world-changing leaders lead with prayer.

A Global Search for Praying Leaders

We don't consider ourselves experts in prayer but rather enthusiasts—eager to learn as we strive to lead fruitful organizations. This posture launched our quest to find what the six-figure research study did not: praying leaders who would let us sit at their feet and learn how to pray like leaders.

We spent more than one hundred hours interviewing leaders across six continents who collectively serve in more than one hundred countries and commissioned a team of researchers to study the prayer lives of leaders in our time and throughout history.

Our *eureka* came when we started studying global leaders, asking them to teach us how to become praying leaders.

Something miraculous, even historic, is happening in the global Church. Missiologists say they have never seen anything like it. Church historians confirm the same.[9] People are coming to Christ, churches are being planted, and communities are being transformed through community development and the Gospel at never-before-seen rates, in challenging places like Iran, Nepal, Afghanistan, India, China, Iraq, and North Africa.

It's happening in our lifetimes: a worldwide revival or reformation on a scale not seen since the earliest days of the Church.

As we started interviewing the diverse leaders behind these movements, the number one principle, practice, and emphasis driving radical transformation—to a person, without exception—is *extraordinary prayer*.

Their leadership secret isn't a "leadership practice" at all: It's a prayer life.

The First Interview

Our very first interview was with a woman named Rosebell, an unsung hero who has served victims of genocide for forty years in a landmine-laden war zone.[10] She is building an extremely effective organization in one of the toughest areas of the world. Most people couldn't withstand this dangerous, soul-draining work for a few months, much less four decades. But Rosebell radiates joy, and she credits her robust prayer life. "Even in a war, Jesus makes me so happy," she said. "When I was young and wanted to tithe, I had no money. The one thing of value I did have was time. I committed to tithe my time and pray and read Scripture and worship for two to two and a half hours every day, *and I've done that for the last forty years.*"

We needed to know if this incredible praying leader was an anomaly or the norm for the global Church, and we wanted to continue the search for people like her in contexts more similar to our own.

We broadened our research to praying leaders in all spheres, from businesses to nonprofits to churches. We interviewed prominent leaders with recognizable names, like Joni Eareckson Tada, Francis Chan, John Mark Comer, John Ortberg, Tim Mackie, Jon Tyson, and Mark Batterson, asking them to share their prayer habits. We researched the well-documented prayer lives of leaders like Christine Caine, Priscilla Shirer, and John Piper. We talked with Christ-following leaders from a host of companies large and small. Finally, we researched the prayer habits of Christian leaders throughout history. Patterns, principles, and commonalities emerged with undeniable clarity.

The Discovery

A billionaire business leader, a war refugee nonprofit leader, and the pastor of a village church nestled among the Himalayan mountains—all had *very similar* prayer practices. But their practices weren't novel; they echoed those of Christian leaders throughout history, from James, the brother of Jesus, to St. Ignatius.

What we found were diamonds: beautiful, transcendent practices shared across the entire spectrum of leadership. We interviewed a New York financier who prays for hours to hear the Holy Spirit before making major business decisions, a pastor investing in prayer and challenging leaders to make prayer "a line item in their budget," a church planter who prayed through the launch of 15,000 churches, and a leader who rallied more than 200,000 people to gather on a mountain exclusively for prayer.

Above all, it became abundantly clear: *An intentional prayer life is the nonnegotiable constant of lasting, fruitful Christian life and leadership.*

Four Common Approaches to Prayer and Leadership

Our research revealed four main approaches to prayer and leadership, which can be represented by a two-by-two grid with one axis for prayerfulness and the other for leadership.

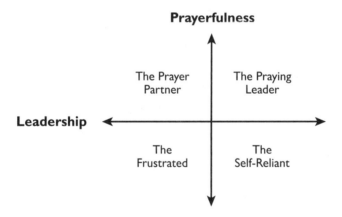

Type 1: The Frustrated—People Not Growing in Prayer or Leadership

This category will get little mention, except to say that those we learned about in this state seemed to be repeating the same mistakes in a cycle of frustration. We found these leaders sought to grow neither in their leadership nor in prayer. They tended to be apathetic toward God or blamed others rather than taking initiative.

Type 2: The Prayer Partner—Intercessors, Praying Believers, Monastics

The people in the second category might be thought of as prayer warriors or prayer partners. These individuals play an essential role in an organization, though they are often outside formal positions of leadership. Intercessors and prayer partners have indeed been *the* catalyst for revival, reformation, cultural renewal, and spreading the Good News of Jesus to the ends of the earth for thousands of years.

Not everyone has formal leadership roles, but *every* believer can pray and model a life of prayer for others. Those who faithfully model prayer can empower everyone they influence to become people of prayer, regardless of position or job title. These leaders of prayer are part of a rich and beautiful tradition of believers of all cultures and stations of life called to "open the heavens" through prayer and pave the way for the Kingdom of God to come in power and beauty. Anna and Simeon in the Advent story prayed for decades for the coming of the Messiah, exemplifying the devotion to prayer that characterizes Type 2, the prayer partners (Luke 2:22–38).

In the global Church, many believers are trained to spend one to two hours a day in personal prayer, Scripture reading, corporate prayer, and worship, regardless of organizational role or responsibility.[11] These communities are practicing extraordinary prayer down to each individual believer.

Another example of a prayer partner is Dorothea Clapp. Late in her life, Dorothea lived across the street from a local high school and wanted to see the students encounter Jesus, but she had no direct contact or relationship with them. So she prayed for every student who walked past her window. One of the people walking by was a rebellious teenage boy named George. She prayed and prayed for George for two years as he walked past her window each day on his way to and from school.[12] George Verwer powerfully met Jesus and went on to start Operation Mobilization (OM), a missionary movement that has touched millions of lives, engaging more than 5,000 workers representing more than one hundred nationalities.[13] Dorothea remained a prayer partner of OM for decades.

It should be mentioned, too, that despite the vital role of prayer partners, we must not simply delegate prayer. This modern practice of outsourcing prayer to staff or volunteers while we pursue other obligations and opportunities of leadership is largely a deception among Western Christians that keeps us from becoming praying leaders.

Jesus *never* taught this, the disciples modeled *the opposite*, and there is no historic church leader who endorsed the idea of delegating prayer only to those deemed most fit for the role of intercessor.

Type 3: The Self-Reliant—Leaders Who Try to Serve God in Their Own Strength and Ability

One nonprofit leader candidly shared, "As I've grown in my leadership roles and responsibilities, my focus and prioritization of prayer have unquestionably decreased." The Barna Group documented this trend in a 2017 study on prayer. They found that college-educated individuals were 20 percent less likely to pray and ask God for guidance than those with only a high school education.[14] And these findings match our experience that well-educated, well-trained, experienced leaders are often less likely to value prayer, model prayer, or invest in prayer than their less *self-reliant* counterparts. As we gain our footing as leaders, we risk losing our dependence on God.

But Jesus modeled the exact opposite.

As the demands and renown of His ministry intensified there are *more* references to Jesus' prayer life. The more weight and responsibility and the larger His following, the *more* He emphasized retreating to solitary places to be alone with God and pray.

Instead of following this example of Jesus, many leaders make an internal "deal" with God. *Lord, You see how busy I am doing Your work. I cannot take time to spend with You, but will You bless all I am doing anyway?* We wouldn't teach or even admit this practice, but it is an internal bargain made in a million different ways.

In our research, we appreciated the candor of well-known, well-respected Christian leaders who confessed to having anemic prayer lives. The data confirms it's an affliction shared by the majority of Christian leaders in our context.

It takes humility to admit we need God's presence so desperately that we would spend time in prayer and seeking, rather than planning and laboring. Many Christian leaders succumb to the great temptation to operate in the bottom right quadrant of "self-reliant leader." Many of these leaders use their God-given charisma and talent to build organizations and advance important causes. But they lead attuned to their own abilities and influence, straining against their limitations rather than seeing limitations as an invitation to seek the One who is limitless.

As their following grows, these leaders push, strive, and promote. Most leadership books we've read train leaders to do *this* more effectively: to manage stress, time, or influence; to strengthen communication or strategy; to mold ourselves until we've become leaders others would want to follow.

These aren't illegitimate pursuits, but neither are they the ultimate pursuit. We think of our children's days in preschool soccer. Many Saturday mornings, we'd stand on the sidelines shouting, "No! Turn around! The goal is the other way!" More than once, our little kickers scored in the wrong net. Amid the swarm of jerseys and shin guards, our kids struggled to remember which goal they were aiming for. Similarly, the swarm of leadership culture can prevent us from seeing that the goal is not influence, productivity, or efficiency, but Jesus. We score, but sometimes in the wrong net.

As we try to squeeze prayer into our busy lives, God stands at the other end of the field, saying, "Turn around! I'm over here; I *am* the goal!" Influence, productivity, and efficiency flow out of our immersion in Christ.

The point of Christian leadership, after all, is still Jesus.

Type 4: The Praying Leader—Growing Leaders Rooted in Dynamic, Growing Prayer Lives

To embrace prayer is not to indiscriminately disregard leadership principles; this is not what we propose. We are practitioners and students of leadership, with advanced degrees from Harvard, Stanford, University of California Berkeley, and St. Thomas. We value education, leadership training, and organizational excellence. But to our core we believe that an overemphasis on leadership and an underemphasis on the presence of Christ can lead to tragedy, personally and organizationally.

We need to discover the beautiful balance of prayer and leadership that the late Scottish theologian John Murray termed "intelligent mysticism," which values both strategic leadership and fervent prayer.

Praying leaders have quit worshiping at the altars of achievement and have shattered the illusion of their self-sufficiency. As a result, they, like Billy Graham, invest in a dynamic, growing prayer life. They trade the striving of the bottom right quadrant for the surrender of the upper right quadrant.

Prayerful leadership invites us to pursue God's priorities over leadership best practices. The praying leaders we learned from prioritize prayerfulness, even at the cost of "productivity," and they truly believe the exchange is worth it. They draw people to Jesus and leave lasting legacies of Kingdom impact as they rely on God, leading from a place of joy, peace, and rest. As they pursue God's presence, heaven shows up fulsomely in their lives and organizations in ways far beyond human capability.

C. S. Lewis's spiritual mentor, Father Walter Adams, instilled in Lewis one simple, life-altering concept: "Look after the roots, and the fruits will look after themselves."[15]

Too often, we can become obsessed with fruit to the point that we neglect our roots. It's madness from an eternal perspective.

We often forgo the strength of heaven and rely on our own ability. We eschew the wisdom of heaven for our own ideas. We rely on our own energy and favor when the energy and favor of heaven are available. All of heaven's resources are available every moment when we stop filling our busy lives beyond capacity in order to be filled with His life, stop pursuing our agendas to receive His guidance, and stop our running to take time to walk with Him.

But our transformation to prayerful leaders does not come quickly. It shouldn't. We have to fight heart and soul for a dynamic prayer life. It will take our whole self.

We've read books on prayer that focus on the inner life. We've read books on leadership that focus on running successful organizations. But we don't want to—or believe we're called to—live this bifurcated life. What might happen if we became not only leaders who pray but, more specifically, praying leaders? How would that change the way we pray, the way we lead, and the spiritual vitality of the organizations we serve?

Two Training Grounds

We found that praying leaders learned to pray mainly on two training grounds. The first is apprenticeship. The best way for a leader to become a praying leader is by learning from other praying leaders: replicating and modifying their habits, postures, prayers, and rhythms. The popular expression "more caught than taught" syncs with this idea of apprenticeship.

To apprentice under praying leaders, we prioritized firsthand interviews and extended observation so we could dig into the lives of these praying leaders, give concrete examples, and awaken a thirst like a deer thirsts for water (Psalm 42:1).

These praying leaders were on a journey to "train their souls," constantly looking for new ways to pray, new prayers to guide them, and new ways to get Scripture into their hearts. They sought to spend more, not less, time in prayer, inventing new ways to remember and connect their souls with God throughout the day, week, and year. These practices, rhythms, and principles of praying leaders became the uniting undercurrents that propelled fruitful, thriving, lasting legacies of leadership.

The second training ground is at the feet of Jesus. There was a fire, beauty, and irresistibility to Jesus' prayer life that drew the disciples to ask Him, "Teach us to pray" (Luke 11:1). They are never recorded asking Him to teach them how to lead, speak, teach, or mentor. But they were compelled to ask Jesus to teach them prayer, because they saw that it was the foundation of Jesus' life and leadership. Jesus often taught the importance of prayer, through both words and actions.

- Could you not pray with me one hour? (Matthew 26:40)
- "Watch and pray so that you will not fall into temptation" (Matthew 26:41).

- "This kind can only come out through prayer" (Mark 9:29).
- Abide in me; without me you can do nothing (John 15:5).
- The Father is always with me (John 8:29).
- "When you pray..." (Matthew 6:5).
- Jesus taught them that they should always pray (Luke 18:1).

It is profound to think that God came to Earth, walked among us, and taught us how to pray. Jesus' prayer life in Scripture forms the core of all the habits we'll explore, and so as we explore each habit, we will dive into its "Jesus origin."

Christian Dawson, a pastor at Bridgetown Church in Portland, Oregon, described it this way: "The people who followed Jesus first were all taken aback by Jesus' prayer life. They were fascinated by it. Jesus woke up early to pray. When He was exhausted, He'd get alone to pray. When He was successful, He'd get away to pray. When He was in trial, He stayed up all night to pray. It's as if the first work and the last work that Jesus was up to was always prayer. Our Rabbi lived something that's so easy to forget: Prayer, more than anything else, fuels our love for God, His people, and His mission in the world."[16]

The disciples had watched Jesus pray and wanted their Rabbi to teach them directly, but we, too, can experience the beauty of learning to pray from our Lord Himself. Jesus is still teaching His leaders to pray. As a 1,500-year-old hymn so beautifully articulates, He is still our "best thought, by day or by night."[17]

Scripture gives us another secret: Jesus is still praying for us right now, because He "lives to intercede" for us, even today (Hebrews 7:25).

Christian leaders do not need another pithy leadership axiom, as if one new insight were so profound it would change the face of Christian leadership. But if Christian leaders were to en masse develop dynamic prayer lives and instill this passion in those they mentor and lead, history and Scripture tell us that neighborhoods and nations would change for generations. As God told Israel, "If my people...humble themselves and pray and seek my face...then I will hear from heaven...and will heal their land" (2 Chronicles 7:14).

The whole of heaven is eagerly waiting for us to get on our knees.

PRAYER

*Dear Jesus, help me to spread Your fragrance everywhere I go. Flood my
soul with Your spirit and love. Penetrate and possess my whole being so
utterly that all my life may only be a radiance of Yours. Shine through
me and be so in me that every soul I come in contact with may feel Your
presence in my soul. Let them look up and see no longer me but only
Jesus. Stay with me and then I shall begin to shine as you shine, so to
shine as to be a light to others.*
Amen.

—Mother Teresa

PRAYER TOOL

Each chapter will end with practical tools to help you lead with prayer. Additional tools and resources are available at www.leadwithprayer.com.

While prayer in a Western context is often thought of as an individual activity, we encourage you to invite friends or colleagues into this pursuit. Who do you know who could help create meaningful changes in your prayer life? Invite them into this process, and consider reading this book together.

Authoring this book as a team has not only increased the joy of writing but also unquestionably helped us with the application. This book was written in community, and we encourage you to read it in community, too.

Lastly, we invite you to pray this book. Stop often and pray when you read an interview that ignites something in your heart. Pray one of the prayers you read. Pray through some of the psalms you see. We issue this invitation with confidence, because most of this content belongs not to us but to the saints we've encountered.

PART I

HOW LEADERS PRIORITIZE PRAYER

CHAPTER 1

LEADERS "WASTE TIME" WITH GOD

The first great and primary business to which I ought to attend every day was, to have my soul happy in the Lord.

—George Müller

Several years ago, I (Ryan) heard a story that has stuck with me ever since. A foreign president arrived early for his scheduled appointment with a South Korean pastor. To the president's great frustration, the pastor's assistant made him wait while the pastor concluded his hour of uninterrupted midday prayer. Nothing was to come between the pastor and this time reserved to be with God.

"Do you know who I am?" the president angrily demanded of the secretary.

The secretary tried to offer some perspective as she calmly replied, "Do you know who he is talking to right now?"

Few leaders adopt the perspective that this pastor and his assistant shared: that no earthly power or pressing demand takes precedence over spending time with the King of Kings.

Leaders have an overabundance of demands on their time. Packed schedules impose a practical barrier to becoming a praying leader. But this practical barrier is rooted in an ideological one: *We forget who we're talking to.*

If we operate under the illusion that we are in control of our schedule, day, or organization, then why pray? If we believe we are in control, then we will struggle to see how prayer could be the best, most effective use of our limited time. Prayer demands that we offer back to God the control that has been His all along.

I (Peter) confess that seeing prayer as a *first priority* has often been a struggle, although I *know* and would be quick to acknowledge the importance of prayer. Slowing down does not come easily, even when there are dedicated times and places for prayer.

Each quarter, HOPE International, where I serve, holds designated days of prayer. I faithfully attend, but on one day of prayer, when facilitators invited our team to find a quiet place for silent prayer, I remember spending my "prayer time" ruminating over the operational and staffing challenges HOPE was facing. I ventured outside for a walk but focused on trying to solve the problems myself.

By the end of the day, I had spent precious few moments in prayer as I paced the grounds. Instead, I found myself fixated on what *I* needed to do: strategizing, planning, and toiling—opting for human effort with a sprinkling of prayer pixie dust. At the end of the day, I had no peace and no clear direction. What I did have, perhaps for the first time, was clarity that I had a prayer problem and erroneous assumptions of who was in control.

The Hour That Saved a Decade

In my (Ryan's) family we frequently recollect and recount one story to remind ourselves who is in control.

When I was a teenager, my dad launched a brand and grew a successful business. After ten years of long days, late nights, and crisscrossing the country, his startup was offered an exclusive deal with a major Fortune 100 company. This was the kind of deal wide-eyed entrepreneurs can only dream about when they eagerly launch their companies.

"Yes!" seemed the obvious answer, but my dad took the matter to prayer, remembering Proverbs 3:6: "In all your ways submit to him, and he will make your paths straight." He prayed about the deal for one hour. With such an attractive offer on the table, that hour of prayer could have been seen as time better spent signing contracts and drafting press releases. But while in prayer, my dad sensed clearly from heaven that he should turn down the deal, though he could not say why.

The Scriptures say, "You will...be led forth in peace" (Isaiah 55:12), and even though this deal looked irresistible on paper, my dad felt the opposite of peace. He turned down the offer. His business partner was livid as he reminded my dad, "This is what you've worked your entire life for!" But my dad held his ground.

Several months later, that same Fortune 100 company surprised Wall Street and the world by declaring bankruptcy after an unforeseen change in the industry. Had my dad signed the deal, this company would have taken his company down with it. That one hour dedicated to the Lord in prayer saved ten years of investment and scores of jobs my dad's company had created.

Ever since that experience, there's been no doubt in our family that time spent with God is never wasted.

The Data on Praying Leaders

Without exception, the praying leaders we interviewed would say that the most productive moments of their life are those spent with Jesus.

In mysterious and wonderful ways, these leaders can recount testimonies of how centering their leadership on prayer exponentially increased their impact, and research supports their anecdotal assertions. A privately commissioned study conducted by the Barna Group revealed encouraging results. Among organizations that prioritize prayer:

- 91 percent of respondents feel more aligned to the mission of the organization;
- 85 percent believe God is more clearly accomplishing His work through the ministry;
- 78 percent agree that they feel "less stressed in [their] day to day responsibilities" due to corporate prayer; and
- 70 percent agree that their "productivity has increased."

The study showed that these effects are especially true in ministries where prayer is corporate rather than individual, mandatory rather than optional, and proactive rather than reactive.[1]

Although we have each seen God work through prayer to accomplish "immeasurably more than all we ask or imagine" (Ephesians 3:20), we offer no guarantees that the input of prayer will yield predictable, desirable outcomes or exponential increases in productivity as we most often conceive of it. Fruitfulness in prayer is far more nuanced than simply receiving our anticipated answer to our requests. Praying leaders would tell us that time spent in prayer *is* productive and fruitful, but even more, time spent in prayer is foundational to the rest of their leadership.

Leading through Minefields

"I was fourteen years old when the bombs started dropping on my village. We all looked for a place to hide. I found a small cave to hide in, but as I climbed in, I saw a poisonous snake right in front of me. Bombs were going off behind me, and a snake was in front of me. I got on my knees and prayed that God would stop the snake—just like He stopped the lions in Daniel—and He did it! The snake never bit me."[2]

Rosebell (whom we introduced in the introduction) shared this story when we asked her about one of her first faith-building answers to prayer. Stories like this one continued as she described forty years of answered prayers, orchestrated by a sovereign God.

Rosebell is like a lesser-known Mother Teresa. She runs a highly effective underground network of leaders who serve children in a war zone, providing food, education, shelter, and safe passage. The situation on the ground is constantly changing, and she spends her days crafting action plans to respond to crisis after crisis. Many leaders can relate to days like these, but Rosebell's crises often involve the tragic intersection of land mines, mortar rounds, and children.

Forty years of leadership in a war zone have not hardened this praying leader. When I (Ryan) first visited the bamboo village where Rosebell resides, fear was palpable. We spent time with victims of land mines, whose bodies had been marred by explosions and whose synapses had been rewired by trauma. Our visit was cut short when we all had to evacuate abruptly because soldiers were within hours of once again reaching the village.

For decades, villagers had lived under this constant threat and uncertainty. So much was out of their control, but in stark contrast to the darkness of death, urgency, injury, fear, and loss that surrounds her, the light of Rosebell's joy shines brightly. She credits the time she spends in God's presence as the source. Since Rosebell decided to tithe 10 percent of her time, beginning at the age of eighteen, extraordinary prayer has been the foundation of her joy-filled ministry.

When her ministry was just beginning, Rosebell received the call that would-be refugees dream of, offering her asylum in a safe country. Rather than assuming this was the gift of God, she took the matter to prayer, and in recurring dreams, she heard directly from Jesus to stay and serve her people.

She started by taking a few children into her home. Now, Rosebell serves thousands of refugee children and trains war refugees to plant churches and to farm. She and the team she's assembled drop seeds of eternal joy and hope in hopeless, dark, and painful places. She is quick to say it is prayer that sustains them.

Seeing Rosebell's enduring faith and joy amid a seemingly impossible situation, we wanted to understand more. "Rosebell, please teach us how to pray like you!" we asked.

Her own rhythm of prayer begins with thirty minutes of solitary prayer on her morning walk. "I go on a walk with Jesus every morning. I'll look at the spider web, and I see its intricate design and beauty, and I think about how Jesus has woven my life with precision and beauty, and I thank Him for these little reminders. Everything reminds me of Jesus. I always look for ways to enjoy Jesus." Following her morning walk, Rosebell engages with her team in prayer for another thirty minutes.

Throughout the day, she takes breaks to pray and receive peace from Jesus. Prayer is woven into her day, as she comes across unexpected moments when someone is in need. As she walks through mine-infested jungles to reach refugee camps, she's aware of the risks but secure in God's control.

In the evening, Rosebell spends time studying Scripture, praying for needs, and writing in her journal. She keeps a prayer book in which she records her prayer requests on one side of a ledger and the corresponding answers on the other. Over the decades, she has filled stacks of these journals, and she's kept them all as tangible reminders of answered prayer to stir her faith and prod her to trust God with her current needs.

A Bouquet amid Bombs

Rosebell recently sent us a photo of a water-filled tarp where her ministry conducted a pop-up baptism in an area in which armed conflict is underway. A bouquet of flowers adorned each corner of the makeshift baptismal. The contrast of a hope-filled baptismal with fresh-cut flowers in the middle of a war zone was like one of Rosebell's reminders of Jesus: He is like fresh-cut flowers in the war zone, joy in the midst of unimaginable trials and tribulations.

Leadership requires not only productivity but also compassion, energy, and vision. Rosebell finds that only friendship with Jesus refreshes her soul. Only discovering God's new mercies and His great faithfulness every morning gives her the strength to carry on with circumstance-defying joy.

Rather than making productivity her goal, the significant time Rosebell "wastes" in friendship with Jesus fills her with such otherworldly joy that she feels "fresh for everything,"[3] in the words of Oswald Chambers. Rosebell's secret to sustained, fruitful service is making time for deep enjoyment of Jesus.

"I would not be able to do it for one day if I did not receive joy from Jesus multiple times throughout the day," she says. Over and over, Rosebell stopped and smiled and told us again, "It's Jesus; He makes me so happy inside, no matter what I face during the day."

Most of us don't serve in an actual war zone, but all forms of leadership can bring compassion fatigue and slowly drain our soul. The stress and pressures of leadership are real, and challenges can increase our adrenaline as though we were under attack. Without regular, vital connection with Christ, we can let the pressures of leadership steal our joy, our strength, our life.

Rosebell's journey of prayer began with commitment, but it progressed to delight. Her example aligns with the conclusions of philosopher and author James K. A. Smith, who writes that we can train our emotion of love, growing to love the rituals we practice. This is true of the praying leaders we met. Their joy in prayer grew as their time in prayer grew.

As one leader told us, "In my life the people who have the most consistent and vibrant prayer lives are those who learned to *actually like* praying." They weren't born with preternatural prayer lives: They *learned* to like praying.

Finding joy in prayer becomes one of the most important, sustaining skills of Christian leadership.

While many of us who are new to leading with prayer might wonder if time in prayer is wasted, the praying leaders we interviewed find such joy, delight, and fruit in their time with the Father that they yearn to "waste time" with God: to be with Him just for the pleasure of it.

A Manhattan Monk

On the surface, it would be hard to imagine a starker contrast to Rosebell's environment than a Manhattan-based investment firm. Yet John Kim, who has managed billions of dollars and holds a PhD from MIT, evidenced similar delight in prayer. John is not driven by productivity and financial return; he is driven by prayer. He founded a house of prayer and entrepreneurship named Coram Deo in the heart of Manhattan (*Coram Deo* translates to "living before the face of God"). It was John who first introduced us to the concept of "wasting time" with God. Initially we were puzzled at the phrase, given how hard we've worked to maximize efficiency and minimize waste in the organizations we lead— but as John went on to describe what he meant, we realized that's what praying leaders like Rosebell had been modeling all along.

As John shared about his prayer practices, he used the example of how good friends get together without any agenda. John is an investor, entrepreneur, pastor, board member, husband, and father of a young son. He can little afford to waste time, yet he blocks ample time every day just to "be with Jesus, with no agenda."[4] The goal is connection, shared experience, and delight. It most certainly is not wasted time; it's a source of joy and wisdom.

John shared about a time when he spent hours in due diligence for an investment. He then took all his research into a time of prayer, spending a couple additional hours "fixing [his] eyes on Christ." He brought his ideas to Jesus, just as one might discuss plans with a friend or a close colleague. In conversation, God refined John's ideas, and the bold, confident investment strategy that emerged worked beyond John's imagination. But when John tells this story, he doesn't highlight the success. The outcome is almost an afterthought. He focuses on the friendship with Jesus and the joy of serving a God who wants to spend time with him. To John, it's the joy of friendship with Jesus that matters.

John describes the transformative moment when he understood the context of God the Father's declaration of delight in Jesus: "This is my Son, whom I love; with him I am well pleased" (Matthew 3:17). It wasn't after the crucifixion, the feeding of the 5,000, or a miraculous healing. The Father declared His pleasure *before* Jesus accomplished anything: before He healed, taught, or led anyone. God is not waiting for us to accomplish a particular target before He is "well pleased."

Similarly, Jesus' first call for His young leaders in training was not to achieve particular outcomes or targets but simply to be with Him: "He appointed twelve that they might *be with him*" (Mark 3:14, emphasis added).

Joy, a Requirement

Ibrahim Omondi, leader of DOVE Africa, oversees churches and ministries throughout eastern and central Africa. It's a demanding role. He could spend his entire year just checking in with the pastors under his oversight, but like Rosebell, his joy is unmistakable, despite the pressures.

"I couldn't go a day without praying," he says. "The joy of the Lord is my strength!"

He chuckles as he quotes Nehemiah 8:10, because he knows it sounds trite, yet for Ibrahim, Rosebell, and other praying leaders, it's true.

"God helps me get above the clouds of discouragement and frustration and ride above those clouds. They are there, yes, but I'm not going to let them weigh me down; I'm looking at the King of Kings, Lord of Lords who is able to deal with each one of those things, and I'm smiling because He's smiling at me."[5]

In Scripture, we are *commanded* to find joy in the Lord (Philippians 4:4), and this command is every bit as direct as the commands instructing us not to commit murder or adultery. Finding our joy in God is no trivial suggestion, as C. S. Lewis implied when he wrote "Joy is the serious business of heaven."[6] G. K. Chesterton spoke similarly when he called joy "the gigantic secret of the Christian."[7]

In case there was any doubt that joy is one of the central goals of prayer, Christ told His leaders in training, "Ask and you will receive, *so that* your joy may be complete" (John 16:24 NRSV, emphasis added).

Jesus derived joy from experiences with His Father, and He sought the same for His followers.

God Winks

Jesus modeled friendship in the little ways He related to the disciples, through something a friend of ours likes to call "God winks." For example, there are millions of ways Jesus could have appeared directly to Peter after His resurrection. But the way Jesus chose to show Himself was to repeat the same miracle where their relationship began (John 21:1–6). It is as if a modern-day screenwriter wrote the scene, complete with a well-executed callback. God's playfulness, joy, and personality are evident in the way Jesus showed Himself in disguise multiple times after the resurrection (Luke 24:13–31; John 20:11–18).

In my (Ryan's) own life, I've experienced these "God winks" and gestures of friendship. When I was nineteen, my dad and I went on a prayer hike in the woods to ask God for direction. We felt we were supposed to take a father–son trip to serve the underground church in a closed communist country. The trip was going to be dangerous, and we wanted to confirm it was God and not our own whims compelling us to go. On the hilltop of a forest clearing, we prayed together. As soon as we said "Amen," a bald eagle flew right over our heads and called out. For us, this was not a superstitious sign but a little wink from heaven, reminiscent of the playfulness of Christ with His disciples.

That trip and the prayer that preceded it led to several miraculous escapes from communist soldiers and the opportunity to help thousands of underground church leaders over many years.

Two decades later I was on the verge of losing my business because of COVID. All of the late nights, risks, money, and stress invested in building a thriving business were evaporating in the span of a few months. I was on my morning prayer walk, but the burden I carried made even walking a challenge. I asked the Lord, "Are we going to make it through this?"

At that moment a bald eagle swooped closely over my head. I'd made that same walk more than a thousand times and never seen an eagle, especially not one soaring a few feet above my head. It was the wink again. It was the love of a Father, not only encouraging but kind…even playful. The joyful reassurance of that moment gave me the strength to continue leading with hope in a season of despair.

Gerald Manley Hopkins wrote a poem about the playfulness of God saying, "Christ plays in ten thousand places":[8] in spider webs and eagles, in fish stories with the disciples, in winks, and smiles on His children.

Friendship Precedes Impact

Christ modeled friendship not only with His followers but also with His Father. He often talked about His close connection with the Father through prayer. Statements like "Father, I thank you that you have heard me," "whatever the Father does the Son also does," and "I pray that they will all be one, just as you and I are one" are rooted in deep friendship and trust (see John 11:41, 5:19, 17:21 NLT).

It's one of the great mysteries of the Christian faith that God traveled through time and space to come among us and sit around a campfire in the desert making friends with a bunch of regular people. Through these friendships, Jesus turned the world upside down without ever leaving a handful of towns.

We haven't heard any leadership guru endorse this friendship-first strategy of "wasting time." Yet God designed our effectiveness to flow out of our friendship with Him: *Abide in me and you will bear fruit* (see John 15:4–5).

We see the same model of friendship with God preceding impact throughout Scripture. David, Moses, and Abraham would make any shortlist of "greatest biblical leaders," yet the Bible honors them not for their many accomplishments but for their friendship with God: calling David "a man after [God's] own heart" (1 Samuel 13:14), saying God spoke to Moses "as one speaks to a friend" (Exodus 33:11), and referring to Abraham as "God's friend" (James 2:23).

Francis Chan's Walk of Friendship

Rosebell's experience in so many ways paralleled the prayer life of author and church planter Francis Chan. When we sat down with Francis, we were amazed at the similarities. Francis is a former megachurch pastor and author of the wildly popular book *Crazy Love*. But several years ago, he walked away from what seemed the pinnacle of success to invest more deeply and undistractedly in his friendship with God.

He speaks often about the preeminence of prayer in his life.

> I like to achieve things, and I like to get things done. And we live in a time where you can get a lot of things done in five minutes. So, the temptation is "Let me do this, let me do this." I have to wake up and say, "No, I'm not going to see who called. I'm not going to see what's waiting for me..." Self-control is "I want to check my messages—see how many things I need to get done today, but I refuse. Because [prayer] is really the only thing I *have* to do."[9]

Francis reminded us prayer is both important and urgent: a "big rock" priority. He told us he would often say to his staff, "Please tell me if you're not spending an hour with the Lord every day so I can fire you and hire someone who will."[10] This is how seriously Francis values prayerfulness in leaders.

When Francis gathers with the other elders in his church, every meeting begins in prayer—and some meetings never move beyond prayer. "Sometimes in the last five minutes we're like, 'Is there anything we needed to talk about real quick?'" He laughs. Then even that turns back to prayer: "Lord, help us with the things we were supposed to talk about."

Prayer is the center of Francis's life and leadership. He notes "the greatest moments in my life" have been communing with God in prayer, because knowing God "is not *part of* Christianity, this *IS* Christianity."[11]

He's developed a particular practice of imagining who he's talking to in prayer before he begins speaking. "I started craving more than just closing my eyes and saying stuff but really picturing who I was speaking to," Francis says. "What is this God like?...I don't even get His very essence, His set apartness, and yet He invites me in to draw near to Him, and He says it's a throne of grace...I take time to just imagine who I'm coming before with everything I know of Scripture, and then talking."

Like Rosebell, Francis likes to "just go out for a walk and pray—just talking to [God], thanking him, worshiping him."[12]

This walk of friendship with God is a common habit of praying leaders around the world. Profoundly, it's part of the restoration of Eden. In the Garden, God would walk with Adam and Eve in the cool of the evening. The walk was abruptly ended by sin and shame.

The next time prayer is mentioned in the Scriptures is Enoch, who "walked with God" (Genesis 5:24 NASB). This was the start of the restoration of the broken friendship between humans and their Creator. Jesus restored the Eden walk, inviting us to walk freely without shame in the presence of our Creator once again.

Every time leaders "waste time" with God in friendship, we are restoring paradise on Earth. The Kingdom refreshes us, flows through us, and refreshes others. And the end result is joy: the kind of joy that helps us lead through a literal or figurative war zone.

A New Habit of Wasting Time with Jesus

Inspired by the example of Rosebell and other praying leaders, I (Ryan) tried this idea of spending time with God just to enjoy Him—and it set a new course for my life. I got on my knees on my bed and told the Lord I just wanted to talk to Him without any agenda. I eventually asked Him, "Jesus, what is on Your heart? What can I pray for?" I heard the name of a country, so I started praying for that country. The strangest thing started happening; I felt a deep passion well up, and I began crying as I prayed for this country. That experience started a journey of eventually working in that country, and thousands of lives have been touched, all from "wasting time" with God.

Now, every Sunday, I have an extended prayer time when I do not ask God for anything. I worship, praise, listen, and meditate, but I don't ask for a single thing. It was incredibly hard at first. I kept finding myself asking for something, praying for this other person, or expressing this need or want. But over time, I learned to crave time with God without any agenda. Inexpressible joy comes from just being with Him. Now I look forward to my day of enjoyment in prayer; it has become a wellspring of joy that carries me through the week like it's carried Rosebell through a war zone.

An Hour of Adoration

Once, when he felt the heaviness of his problems rather than the joy of God's presence, renowned theologian and author Henri Nouwen sought spiritual direction from Mother Teresa. He retells the encounter: "I remember I was visiting Mother Teresa in Rome. Everyone wanted to talk to her, and I wanted to see her too. I went there as I had some problems. I had some personal struggles—quite a few, actually—and I wanted to ask Mother Teresa how to deal with that. I brought all my stuff to her…I just talked about all my problems."

"Then she looked at me and said, '…If you spend one hour a day in adoration of your Lord and never do anything that you know is wrong, you'll be fine.'…Obviously, she didn't say anything that I didn't know, but suddenly it hit me as so true and so coming from the right place that that little word was enough for me."[13]

It begs the question, what does an hour of adoration look like for Mother Teresa? As she explained it to one reporter, it looks like "wasting time" with God.

"When you pray, what do you say to God?" the reporter asked.

"I don't say anything," she replied. "I listen."

"What does He say?" the reporter shot back eagerly.

"He doesn't say anything. He listens. And, if you don't understand that, I can't explain it to you."[14]

She later wrote, "Everything starts from prayer. Without asking God for love, we cannot possess love, and still less are we able to give it to others…To be able to bring His peace, joy, and love, we must have it ourselves, for we cannot give what we have not got."[15]

Joy Is Strategic for Leaders

University of California Berkeley did a large and expansive study on the effect of "awe" on our brains, particularly spiritual awe, something Christians would call the "joy of the Lord." When humans experience transcendent awe, synapses fire in our brain causing us to be measurably:

- more humble
- more patient
- more connected to others
- more kind
- more generous

We also experience:

- increased critical thinking
- better moods
- a decreased sense of materialism[16]

It's like awe in worship literally leads to the fruit of the Spirit in our lives, and it's scientifically measurable. These qualities help us lead like Jesus and make us a blessing to those we lead.

Slowing down to "waste time" with God is about the hardest thing a leader can do in this busiest of ages of humankind. But praying leaders live the words of the hymn "In the Garden," "The joy we share, as we tarry there, none other has ever known."[17] It takes a commitment to "tarry," yet time spent together is the foundation of friendship, and friendship with Jesus is the foundation of Christian leadership.

Praying leaders across time and around the world have learned the secret of "wasting time" in God's presence, and as a result generations have been changed.

PRAYER

*Late have I loved you, O Beauty ever ancient, ever new, late have I
loved you!*

*You were within me, but I was outside, and it was there that I searched
for you.*

*In my unloveliness I plunged into the lovely things which you created.
You were with me, but I was not with you. Created things kept me
from you; yet if they had not been in you they would have not been
at all.*

*You called, you shouted, and you broke through my deafness.
You flashed, you shone, and you dispelled my blindness. You
breathed your fragrance on me; I drew in breath and now I pant
for you.*

*I have tasted you, now I hunger and thirst for more. You touched me,
and I burned for your peace.*

—St. Augustine

PRAYER TOOL

WALK WITH GOD GUIDE

Like Francis Chan and Rosebell, many of the leaders we interviewed use a daily walk to "waste time" with God and build upon their friendship.

Recent studies have shown that walking is one of the healthiest activities you can engage in for your mind, body, brain, and spirit.

Mental Health

Walking connects the right and left hemispheres of your brain, helping your brain get "unstuck." It releases endorphins and fires up your neurotransmitters, providing greater clarity of thought.

Body Health

Taking a single step moves more than 200 bones and 600 muscles in the human body, pushes blood through the cardiovascular system, and fires up the nervous system to keep you loose.

Brain Health

Walking regularly improves memory, fights rigidity in your brain, and helps long-term brain function and health in myriad ways.

Spiritual Health

Most saliently, walking with God and praying is one of the easiest ways to expand your prayer life. You are engaging both sides of your brain in communion with God. So, regardless of your default brain dominance, your whole self can engage with God in prayer.

HELPFUL TIPS TO WALK AND PRAY

- Verbally invite Jesus to join you on a walk.
- Take a Scripture with you and memorize it.
- Read a psalm several times over on a walk.
- Listen to a worship song while you walk.

- Look at nature around you and compliment God on its beauty.
- Take time to listen.
- Repeat a simple phrase several times, like "God, I need You," "Jesus, I love You," or "Hallelujah."
- Share your worries, fears, frustrations, anxieties, challenges, and struggles.
- Share your hopes, your dreams, what excites you, and what energizes you.
- Take time to pray for anyone you see on the walk to experience Christ.
- Reflect on your life, your family, and your ministry, and offer everything into Christ's hands.

Find ways to enjoy and find joy in Jesus. Joy and friendship with Jesus are the lasting foundations of Christian leadership.

CHAPTER 2

LEADERS TRAIN THEIR SOUL

Pray...with all kinds of prayers.

—Ephesians 6:18

As an NFL chaplain with the Miami Dolphins, Terry Boynton has worked with some of the greatest athletes alive.

The football players he mentors are constantly looking for a training edge, whether it's consuming precise amounts of protein within a prescribed time frame after a workout, bench-pressing with laser timers to track explosiveness in microseconds, or finding their ideal weight for the apex balance of power and speed—anything to give them a slight advantage in competition.

Athletes adopt a technique, refine their training, and find the sweet spot of their body's personal response. Then they repeat the process, over and over. They are constantly training their bodies, but Terry encourages the athletes he mentors to apply that same level of discipline to training their souls in prayer. It's profound for these athletes to think of pouring that much effort and intentionality into their prayer lives. With Terry's help, they've started approaching prayer and discipleship with serious focus and commitment, creating a plan for their prayer lives as they would for their physical training.

It isn't just athletes who benefit from that level of intentionality in their prayer lives. As we spent time with praying leaders around the world, we witnessed and heard about commitment and a purposeful pursuit of greater depths in their relationship with God. These leaders shared and lived the words of King David, "My soul *followeth hard* after thee" (Psalm 63:8 KJV, emphasis added).

With creativity and focus, prayer was woven into leaders' days, weeks, and years. They experimented with different prayer rhythms and practices, adopting a variety of techniques and approaches to cultivate a personal rhythm that included morning devotions, prayer retreats, prayer meetings, evening prayers, prayer lists, and ancient prayers. They were committed and practicing *all of the above.*

If this sounds a bit extreme, one of the most respected biblical leaders went even further: He was willing to die for his prayer rhythms.

Daniel was a young Jewish man, taken into captivity in Babylon. Recognized for his wisdom, he went on to become the chief of staff of the largest empire the world had ever seen. His responsibility wasn't just over a country, but *countries.* But then jealous colleagues came up with a plan to orchestrate his demise, using Daniel's dedication to prayer against him. As the Bible recounts, Daniel chose a den of lions over modifying his prayer practices (Daniel 6).

In a dramatic story with actual ravenous lions, we can easily miss the intensity of Daniel's leadership pressures and his commitment to his prayer life in his personal schedule. Had he just chosen to pray on his morning walk silently to himself, there would have been no lions to contend with. But all of it—the routine, the posture of kneeling, the frequency of getting alone with God multiple times a day—was so important to Daniel that he would rather die than lead without his particular prayer rhythms.

Both Daniel and the leaders we interviewed model what has for centuries been known as a Rule of Life. It's a concept born out of fourth-century Christianity and practiced by hundreds of millions of Christians for more than 1,500 years.

As a very old concept, there are many definitions, but author Marjorie Thompson offers this helpful framework: "A rule of life is a pattern of spiritual disciplines that provides structure and direction for growth in holiness."[1] Stated simply, it's a training plan to grow closer to Christ.

On the importance of a Rule of Life, one leader wrote, "The devil defeats most praying before it happens because we didn't make a plan."[2]

Another praying leader described his Rule of Life this way: "I set my prayer life, then I organize the rest of my life around it."

Ancient Made New

John Mark Comer, author of *The Ruthless Elimination of Hurry* and founding pastor of Bridgetown Church in Portland, Oregon, has a passion to bring ancient spiritual disciplines to the twenty-first century. This passion has grown into the nonprofit Practicing the Way, where he creates resources for discipleship and spiritual formation in post-Christian contexts.

After many years helping Christian families and foundations find amazing, off-the-beaten-path giving opportunities, I (Cameron) now have the privilege of working alongside John Mark as executive director of Practicing the Way. In evaluating and identifying ministries, I noticed that the most fruitful ministries are also the most prayerful. Having observed the correlation between prayer and impact, I now work with John Mark to revive and renew centuries-old Christian spiritual disciplines and practices like prayer in our hurried, overstimulated culture. Our work aims to help followers of Christ become disciples who impact their own corners of the world.

John Mark and I believe in a balance between the rhythm of scheduled and spontaneous prayer practices. Christian tradition would call these two approaches "fixed-hour prayer" and "practicing the presence of God." On fixed-hour prayer, John Mark said, "Following Jesus has to make it on to your schedule, or the odds are it will not happen or it will be sporadic at best."[3]

Ask John Mark about a Rule of Life, and he quotes Dallas Willard, "You must arrange your days so that you are experiencing deep contentment, joy, and confidence in your everyday life with God."[4]

John Mark's Rule of Life includes morning, noon, and evening practices, modeled on the words of David in Psalm 55:17, when he calls upon the Lord at those regular intervals. He explained how he wakes up in the morning, reads a psalm, and listens to God in prayer. He's formed the habit of asking God, "What would please You today?" and then he takes the time to listen for God's reply. Scripture reading is incorporated in different ways throughout the day, from study to devotional to praying Scripture.

Midday, John Mark slips out of his office for a brief walk. He prays the Lord's Prayer and prays through prayer cards that name people, dreams, organizations, and issues John Mark is regularly lifting up to God. In the evening, he does the *Examen*, a prayer in which he Replays, Rejoices, Repents, and Resolves.[5]

These scheduled, extended times every day create a foundation for all the other spiritual practices in John Mark's Rule of Life.

Praying Fast and Slow

In the blockbuster book *Thinking Fast and Slow*, professor of psychology Daniel Kahneman details two primary mental states or two ways we experience our world.

The first state is fast thinking, our default mode. It's a state in which we're thinking quickly. We don't have time to reflect, so we're mainly just reacting to stimuli. In our fast-paced world, we spend most of our time in this mental state. But this default state is deeply informed by the second state.

The second state is slow thinking. This state is one in which we reflect on a problem or even on our thoughts themselves. This type of thinking takes time, effort, and intentionality. Strategy, life-changing decisions, analysis, and reflection are all done in our slow-thinking state.[6]

The real revelation of Kahneman's book is that when we are in the slow-thinking state, we are actually forming and shaping how we are going to think when we are in our fast-thinking state of mind. For example, if we were to realize during a time of reflection and slow thinking that we interrupt people when they talk, we would resolve to catch ourselves when we're in fast mode. Eventually our habit would change as we applied our slow-thinking realization to our fast-thinking default state.

There are volumes of neuroscience behind this phenomenon: Slow thinking taps into a whole different section of our brain. The synapses literally fire differently. We know that great leaders learn to train their default state through scheduled times of thinking slowly, deliberately, and intentionally. This kind of training applies equally to prayer.

Drawing from the Well

Most Christians learn how to pray fast. We learn to pray fast when we bless a friend or a meal, ask for help, give quick praise, or continually remind ourselves of the presence of Jesus. However, the fast prayers gain great strength and power from our seasons of "praying slow," just as fast thinking is informed by our slow thinking. Praying slow is what we call a "prayer time" in the morning, evening, or—like many of the leaders we interviewed—both morning *and* evening.

We fill the well of our hearts when we slow down with a time of intentional prayer each day; we draw from that well in our quick prayers throughout the day.

Perhaps the best historic example of slow praying giving power to quick prayers throughout the day was when Jesus raised His friend Lazarus from the dead. Lazarus had been dead four days when Jesus arrived at the home Mary and Martha had shared with their brother. Having seen Jesus work miracles, the gathered crowd seemed reproachful toward Jesus' delayed arrival. "Could not he who opened the eyes of the blind man have kept this man from dying?" (John 11:37). They thought if only Jesus had been there, things might have turned out differently.

But even before His arrival, Jesus was fulfilling His promise that "this sickness will not end in death" (John 11:4). Jesus had already spent extended time praying and had received God's grace to raise Lazarus earlier. We know this because when Jesus came to the tomb, His only prayer was "Father, I thank you that you have heard me" (John 11:41). Then, as Jesus beckoned him, Lazarus walked out of the grave.

Recently I (Ryan) was at the National Prayer Breakfast in a breakout session for business leaders. A French Canadian businessman stood up to pray. He was a wise and accomplished leader with thousands of employees. But what most affected the room was his prayer—more specifically, the single word he prayed.

He closed his eyes and uttered just the word *Jesus*. The reality of Jesus in that moment was so overwhelming that individuals in the room were moved to tears. It was undeniable that this man had spent a lot of time with Jesus. In just one word, just one mention of the name of Jesus, the room filled with the presence of God, and he did not need to say another word.

Saying the name Jesus and pausing was a fast prayer for this leader, but the power of that moment came from his deep well of extended slow praying for years.

The more we practice slowing-down types of prayer, the more connected we feel to God in the fast-thinking mode of our days as we're tapping into our intuition to solve problems and move initiatives forward. In extended prayer times, the Spirit of God animates our frailties and slowly forms treasure out of clay. As in creation, prayer is where dust and Spirit collide and life is created.

From Habit to Identity

There is a difference between someone who golfs occasionally and a *golfer* or someone who sings sometimes and a *singer*. Likewise, there's a difference between someone who complains occasionally and a *complainer*.

Through repetition, the things we do become a part of our identity.

In the psalms, for example, David's habit of praying to God transforms him from someone who occasionally prays to "a man of prayer" (Psalm 109:4): a man who prays so regularly that it shapes his identity. It's who he is, and it gives him confidence in his relationship with God.

This concept is baked into the Greek language, the language of the New Testament. To describe someone doing something habitually, Greek grammar would say that the person literally *is* that thing. Instead of saying "She golfs," the Greek would say "She *is* golf." Our English translation would be "She is a golfer."

Luke used this idea when he described Jesus' prayer life. "Jesus Himself would *often* slip away to the wilderness and pray" (Luke 5:16 NASB). The Greek implies that Jesus did this so often it was a part of who He was.

The sentence could be translated "Jesus was a *slip away and pray-er.*"

Jesus wasn't a leader who prayed occasionally; He was a praying leader.

Prayer Positively Changes Our Brain

Andrew Newberg, an agnostic neuroscientist at Thomas Jefferson University and Hospital, has been lauded as one of the "30 Most Influential Neuroscientists Alive." He's authored several books, including *How God Changes Your Brain*, and done extensive research scientifically documenting the effects of prayer on the human brain. His work is heralded in diverse publications, from NPR[7] to medical journals.[8] Here's what he concluded:

> Biologically, regular extended prayer over an 8-week period can change the brain to such an extent that it can be measured on a brain scan.[9]

Prayer fortifies or builds new neural pathways in areas of the brain associated with social interaction, compassion, and sensitivity to others. Regular prayer also decreases anxiety, stress, and depression in scientifically measurable ways, positively changing our neurochemistry.[10] Consistent extended prayer also works against anger and rigidity in the brain by reducing stress hormones.[11]

Neuroscientist Richard Davidson, professor of psychology and psychiatry at the University of Wisconsin–Madison and the founder and director of the Center for Healthy Minds, says, "You can sculpt your brain just as you'd sculpt your muscles if you went to the gym. Our brains are continuously being sculpted, whether you like it or not, wittingly or unwittingly."[12]

Newberg expands this idea. "If you want to be good at crossword puzzles, you can practice them and get better at crossword puzzles, but it doesn't make you good at other things. But prayer seems to have the same effect weight lifting has for your body in that it allows you to do other sports, activities, and motions better as you get larger muscles."[13]

This might raise the question, "Doesn't any act of mindfulness produce these same benefits?" Studies show it does not. Kenneth Pargament of Bowling Green State University in his research[14] controlled for mindfulness alone versus prayer and found significant positive differences in mental and physical health in various situations when people prayed versus when they practiced mindfulness or materialistic meditation.[15]

It doesn't happen right away, but prayer physically changes the nervous system in measurable ways.

Just like lifting weights for five minutes one time won't make anyone stronger, starting a prayer habit won't bring instant results. But lifting for thirty to sixty minutes over several months will bring significant physical transformation. The same is true of a prayer life. Over time, things change in us and in our perception of the world.

Scripture creates a powerful parallel between physical training and spiritual training, and recent revelations in neuroscience confirm what the Bible has affirmed for thousands of years: There is physical training and there is soul training, and both are profoundly measurable and reproducible.

Cross-Training

There is a beautiful interaction between routine and variety, which keeps a routine fresh. Athletes call this cross-training, and weight lifters term it *muscle confusion*. Mixing up a routine is more beneficial to the body than doing the same workout routine every week. The same is true for our soul, as the apostle Paul implies when he encourages us to pray "all kinds of prayers" (Ephesians 6:18). As a sample, here are some of the many types of prayers the Bible teaches and praying leaders practice:

Meditating on Scripture (Psalm 1:2)

Journaling (Psalm 102:18)

Delight (Psalm 1:2)

Whispering (1 Samuel 1:13)

Confession (Psalm 51)

Lifting hands (Psalm 141:2)

Clapping hands (Psalm 47:1)

Bowing down (Psalm 95:6)

Kneeling (Psalm 95:6)

Singing (Psalm 5:11)

Shouting (Psalm 98:4)

Praising (Psalm 145:2)

Seeking (Psalm 27:8)

Waiting (Psalm 27:14)

Intercession (1 Timothy 2:1)

Petition (Philippians 4:6)

Listening (Psalm 25:14)

Cross-training in our prayer life takes daily commitment and creativity. But we don't start out as professional weight lifters or NFL athletes. We start small with the goal of gaining strength. We map out a day with God, then expand it.

Shalom's Soul Training

One of the best examples of prayer cross-training came from our friend Shalom in Ethiopia.[16] Shalom runs one of the most dynamic and effective church-planting movements in the world today. He started planting churches, and these churches started planting churches, and today there are more than 15,000 churches in countries people thought were impossible to reach. It's a modern-day book of Acts movement unfolding.

Shalom will say the entire movement is built on a foundation of prayer. He says, "When we are not praying, *we* work. But when we are praying, God's working." When Shalom's team gets together for leadership retreats, the first day is reserved completely for prayer. Only after spending a full day in prayer do they move on to planning.

Shalom told us, "A leader without prayer is like a bird trying to fly without full wings. There is a lot of flapping but no flight. A lot of activity but no lasting fruit."

Shalom maps out his daily prayer life like this:

I start my morning prayer time with a lot of singing, a lot of being immersed in worship. The Lord gives me songs, and God immerses me in His presence. Sometimes I play soft music to get me into the presence. The goal is to really be in awe of the greatness of God. When I see how big God is, I see how incompetent I am, what a sinner I am, that I need forgiveness. So then I take some time to confess my sins and connect my soul to Jesus.

The Bible says there's an enemy who distracts and an enemy who wants to kill, steal, and destroy…So I pray Ephesians 6, the armor of God. In the name of Jesus, I pray against demonic attacks.

After that, I pray for the country, the families, the individuals in ministry.

Then back to worship. All out loud. Praying out loud keeps you alert and awake.

Morning, Noon, Evening

Virtually all the praying leaders we studied and interviewed had plans for their daily, weekly, and yearly prayer rhythms, both personally and professionally. Here are just a few examples.

Morning Prayer

Dallas Willard, philosopher and best-selling author, spoke out Psalm 23 while still in bed to awaken his soul to the beautiful love of God.

Mark Batterson, lead pastor of National Community Church and author of *The Circle Maker*, begins his morning with journaling and Scripture.

Tim Mackie, co-founder of BibleProject, starts the day with his hands open to heaven, quieting his soul and listening to God.

Francis Chan and Rosebell take a walk in the morning, experiencing little tastes of heaven.

I (Ryan) have been deeply impacted by the habit of rolling out of bed directly onto my knees every morning and praying different psalms and ancient prayers to awaken a thirst for God and connect with Him before my day begins.

The morning practices are designed to lift our heart, eyes, and soul to heaven; to remind ourselves of the love of God that can flow through us to impact others throughout the day.

Noon Prayer

Like John Mark Comer, many praying leaders pause at midday or set reminders throughout the day to reorient themselves back to God. Instead of detailing an expansive list here, we will explore these plans and prompts in Chapter 3.

Evening Prayer

Many leaders we encountered had practices and traditions for evening prayer as well. Some of the most common were:

- The *Examen*—a prayer practice of reflecting, repenting, and receiving
- Cleansing Prayer—a prayer cleansing the soul of all that built up during the day and releasing everything to the Lord
- Evensong—evening praise and gratitude

Creating a Rule of Life for Prayer

Without a training plan, an athlete might lift a little here or there but most likely won't be significantly changed by the process. But even a simple plan can help to create a powerful workout. One goal of this book is to function as a personal trainer in prayer, helping leaders create a set of prayer practices to include in their Rule of Life. We've provided a simple table at the end of this chapter to note specific practices to try daily, weekly, and annually.

The praying leaders we encountered dedicated blocks of time that totaled around one to two hours throughout the day for Scripture reading and individual or group prayer. However they've chosen to divide the time, that extended time is reserved to slow down and pray, giving them time to be filled with joy in the presence of God, to fight and persevere in prayer for those they lead, to meditate on Scripture, and to pray all kinds of prayers.

As Terry, the NFL chaplain, explains:

> For many people, the idea of spending hours in prayer would seem like stepping out the door and running a marathon. There is nowhere near the endurance, muscle memory, focus, and lung power to run a marathon without training. But for most of us, the strength is there to run a challenging first mile. With the proper training program, most humans can train up to a marathon much faster than they would have thought possible, just by following a plan.

The Journey of a Praying Leader

There is a three-step journey we observed in praying leaders who have moved beyond merely paying lip service to prayer. Each part of this book maps to a different phase on this journey.

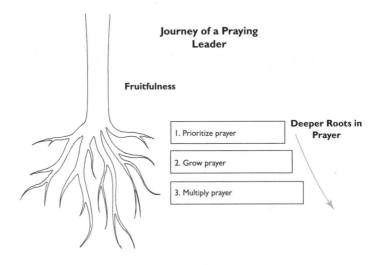

Journey of a Praying Leader

Fruitfulness

1. Prioritize prayer

2. Grow prayer

3. Multiply prayer

Deeper Roots in Prayer

1. Prioritize prayer and begin to build a consistent set of prayer practices as part of a Rule of Life, guarding prayer time and learning to enjoy it.
2. Engage in a variety of prayer practices to grow in relationship with God and begin to model a life of prayer.
3. Invest in building a culture of prayer, multiplying prayer in your organization.

The framework intentionally progresses downward to reflect the humble journey of becoming a deeply rooted person of prayer: a leader who "focuses on the roots."

Most of us are in steps 1 or 2 and are ready to sink our roots more deeply into prayer, learning to become people of prayer. We are eager to discover what praying leaders have found throughout the centuries: The infinite joy of Christ and the resources of heaven are available to us, waiting for us to make room.

PRAYER

Jesus, conqueror of this world,
Help me overcome this world of pride
And live in humility.
Help me overcome this world of pleasure
And find joy in Your presence.
Help me overcome this world of greed
And live in simplicity.
Help me overcome this world of achieving
And live in obedience.
Help me overcome this world of fear
And live in peace.

Help me overcome this world of selfishness
And give up my rights.
Help me overcome this world of darkness
And live in pure light.
Help me overcome this world of hate
And deeply, daily love people.
Help me overcome a world of anger
And live in kindness.
Help me overcome this world of gossip
And rest in silence.
Help me overcome a lazy world
And live with discipline.
Help me overcome a world that has forgotten You
And live in daily gratefulness.

You conquered all temptation and live in me.
Rise up, my God.
Be strong in my heart and overcome,
For the greatest challenge I will face
Lies in my own deceitful desires.
To help me overcome this world,
please destroy my desire for it.
I want to be single of heart, only longing for You,
My Christ, my captain.

—*Ryan Skoog*

PRAYER TOOL

PRAYER MAP

Every workout plan begins with a commitment to try *something*. To help you develop a plan, we have created a customizable tool to create your own Rule of Life.

Don't think of these practices as written in stone. Even by the end of this book you may identify other strategies you'd like to try or different rhythms that help you connect regularly with God.

Over time God will use your prayer practices, and the rest of your Rule of Life, to transform you, even defining your leadership. You will move from a leader who prays to a *praying leader*.

	SUNDAY	MONDAY	TUESDAY	WEDNESDAY	THURSDAY	FRIDAY	SATURDAY
THEME							
PSALMS							
PRACTICES							
MORNING PRAYERS							
MIDDAY PRAYERS							
EVENING PRAYERS							
SCRIPTURE							

Here is an example of my (Ryan's) personal map:

	SUNDAY	MONDAY	TUESDAY	WEDNESDAY	THURSDAY	FRIDAY	SATURDAY
THEME	Worship & gratefulness	Family	Work & ministry	Confession & listening & forgiveness	Nations & the poor	Salvation Friday	Growth & character
PSALMS	Psalm 19, 84, 148	Psalm 63, 112	Psalm 27, 91	Psalm 25, 51	Psalm 10, 67	Psalm 34, 103	Psalm 139
PRACTICES	Read through hymns & worship songs	Pray for & speak blessings over entire family	Pray for staff, companies, work, & goals	Repentance of sinful thoughts, actions, & neglect	Gospel reaches the nations, persecuted church, missionaries	Pray for: family, friends, neighbors, coworkers	Fruit of the Spirit, Beatitudes, Armor of God
	Confess realities of the Gospel & truths of Scripture	Pray a written prayer for each member	Pray for leadership in church & nation	Listen for God's prayer list—pray for whoever comes to mind	Pray for the poor & oppressed nearby & around the world	Pray for opportunities to share your faith with others	Pray for the character of Christ to be formed in you
MORNING PRAYERS	Praise & gratefulness list	Ephesians 1, Ephesians 3	Lord's Prayer, Lorica of St. Patrick	Forgiveness prayer, surrender prayer	Colossians 1	Philippians 1, Ephesians 1	Prayer of St. Francis
MIDDAY PRAYERS	One-sentence prayers & praises	One-sentence prayers & praises	One-sentence prayers & praises	One-sentence prayers & praises	One-sentence prayers & praises	One-sentence prayers & praises	One-sentence prayers & praises
EVENING PRAYERS	Communion, *Examen*, worship	Communion, *Examen*, worship	Communion, *Examen*, worship	Communion, *Examen*, worship	Communion, *Examen*, worship	Communion, *Examen*, worship	Communion, *Examen*, worship
SCRIPTURE	Reading plan, daily Proverb	Reading plan, daily Proverb	Reading plan, daily Proverb	Reading plan, daily Proverb	Reading plan, daily Proverb	Reading plan, daily Proverb	Reading plan, daily Proverb

CHAPTER 3

LEADERS PRACTICE THE PRESENCE OF GOD

The first and most basic thing we can and must do is to keep God before our minds.

—*Dallas Willard*

A few hundred years ago, a dishwasher in a small French abbey tried something revolutionary: spending every possible minute aware of the presence of God.

He never led a large team or received a degree, but he influenced millions of lives through a series of letters he wrote detailing his practice of moment by moment fixing his thoughts, words, and attention on Christ. He called this experience of praying throughout the day "practicing the presence of God." His collected letters have become one of the best-selling Christian books of all time throughout the world.[1]

While, of course, Brother Lawrence had times dedicated solely to prayer—sometimes hours each day—something powerful happened after he finished his scheduled prayer time.

It spilled out into his everyday life.

Brother Lawrence practiced bringing Jesus into every moment, into every normal task, into every act of kindness or service. He remained in an attitude of prayer throughout his days, praying constantly. He lived out the timeless Celtic prayer, "God be in my head."

It was as though he refused to say "Amen" or hang up the phone. He took his prayerful heart posture from the prayer room to the kitchen and the cobbler's bench. He would teach others this practice, encouraging, "We should establish ourselves in a sense of God's presence, by continually conversing with Him."

How would he speak to God? "In the greatest simplicity, speaking to Him frankly and plainly, and imploring His assistance in our affairs, just as they happen."

The fruit of this practice in Lawrence's life was a carefree bliss and what he called a "habitual, silent, and secret conversation of the soul with God, which often causes in me joys and raptures inwardly."

When exposed to Brother Lawrence's ideas for the first time, the spiritual leader Henri Nouwen remarked, "They seemed simple, even somewhat naive and unrealistic."

But with time and reflection, Nouwen reached the opposite conclusion and later wrote, "Brother Lawrence's advice...is not just a nice idea for a seventeenth-century monk, *but a most important challenge to our present-day life situation.*"[2]

Modern-day leaders are still learning how to accept God's seemingly simple invitation to abide in Him as we live out our days.

The CEO and the Dishwasher

Life in the continual presence of God is fully available, not just to Jesus or to seventeenth-century monks but to normal people like us...or even one of the busiest leaders on earth: the CEO and founder of Hobby Lobby, David Green.

On the surface, David's life bears few similarities to that of a country dishwasher. Hobby Lobby is one of the largest companies on the planet, with billions of dollars in annual revenue and tens of thousands of employees. We toured their headquarters; the buildings sprawled onward for more than a mile. Hobby Lobby has so many employees that the company has built its own care clinic as part of its employee health care plan.

As David showed us Hobby Lobby's facilities, his passion for Jesus came through even more clearly than his passion for the company.

We were able to ask David about his prayer life, and he thoughtfully described his journey of practicing the presence of God.

It was profound to hear the leader of one of the world's largest private companies[3] describe experiences so similar to Brother Lawrence's. He talked about trying to "stay aware of God's presence throughout the day" and "keep an ongoing conversation with the Lord" in his office.[4]

Prayer is a defining mark of his leadership. One of the most profound milestones in David's journey of prayer happened early in Hobby Lobby's history when the company was still small and struggling financially. As David flew home from a convention where several missionaries had shared a need for biblical literature, God prompted him to step out in faith to meet this need. "I was looking out the airplane window when something unusual happened. It seemed a quiet voice inside of me said, 'You need to give $30,000 for literature.'"[5]

David didn't have $30,000, but in faith, he mailed four checks for $7,500 each, postdated to span the next four months.[6] David writes:

> When the church staff member on the other end called to acknowledge my gift, he made an intriguing comment. "The day your letter was postmarked," he said, "was the very day that four African missionaries had a special prayer meeting for literature funds. Looks like God answered their prayer!"[7]

This confirmation lit a fire in David. He knew he had heard the voice of God, and he wanted to keep the conversation going.

Like David Green, David the ancient king of Israel describes a similar practice of ongoing connection: "I have set the Lord always before me" (Psalm 16:8 NKJV). The word he used, *set*, is an action verb. It's something we continually *make an effort* to do. It means David Green, Brother Lawrence, and King David all took time, effort, and intentionality to keep God "in their heads."[8]

In our research, practicing the presence of God was the second most prevalent habit; only scheduled prayer times were more common and core to praying leaders' personal rhythms. In varying language, so many of the leaders we interviewed described this same principle:

- "When we're praying, when we're talking to the Father, we open the day in prayer and don't say, 'Amen.' We leave the phone off the hook all day."
- "My fellowship with the Holy Spirit is constant. I'm praying on the go."
- "I'm always speaking to Jesus, and I carry my prayer room during the day."
- "It's a minute-by-minute basis. 'Father, what do You think?'"
- "Pray all the time. Every day, every time you do your work, you stay in the mode of prayer. You're connected to heaven."

These leaders live out the "abiding" that Jesus modeled and invites us into.

How Did Jesus Practice the Presence of God?

In Luke 11:1, the disciples ask Jesus to teach them to pray. Their request prompts the now-famous "Lord's Prayer," but in the context preceding the prayer, it's fascinating to see how the disciples *perceived* Jesus' prayer life:

> One day Jesus was praying in a certain place. When he finished...
> (Luke 11:1)

Even though Luke uses the word *finished* here, Jesus was never truly finished praying. He lived with the reality of God always before Him, and His conversation with the Father was ongoing. His every action imitated the Father's actions: "Very truly I tell you, the Son can do nothing by himself; he can do only what he sees his Father doing" (John 5:19). And His every moment was spent with the Father: The Father "is with me; he has not left me alone, for I always do what pleases him" (John 8:29).

In dialogue, Jesus had one eye on His conversation partner and one on the Father. In listening to people, Jesus had one ear attuned to their words and one ear listening to the Father. He had moments of focused verbal prayer, but He also modeled a permeating life of prayer.

Jesus tells us that this act of abiding through ongoing connection with the Father is not just a merit badge for spiritual overachievers. Since the only path to fruit is to "remain" in Jesus, we need to learn how to do this!

How the Early Church Practiced the Presence of God

The apostle Paul provides another model of praying continually:

> For this reason, since the day we heard about you, *we have not stopped praying for you. We continually ask God* to fill you with the knowledge of his will through all the wisdom and understanding that the Spirit gives. (Colossians 1:9, emphasis added)

Since Paul was praying continually, it was natural for him to encourage others to pray with him. He peppers challenges to pray throughout every letter canonized in Scripture.

- "Devote yourselves to prayer" (Colossians 4:2).
- "Pray in the Spirit on all occasions" (Ephesians 6:18).
- "Pray continually" (1 Thessalonians 5:17).

When Paul says, "Pray continually," he uses the word *adialeiptos*, from the Greek verb *dialeipo*, which means to leave an interval or gap between something. The prefix *a* in *adialeiptos* negates the meaning of *dialeipo*, so Paul is saying literally that there should be no intervals or gaps in your prayer time. Pastor and author J. D. Watson writes that *adialeiptos* "was used in Roman times for a nagging cough; while the person didn't cough every moment, he would still cough often, so it could be said of him, 'He's still coughing.'"[9]

That's the kind of pray-ers we want to become: people who pray and, throughout the day, are still praying.

Practicing the Presence of God Is a Process

Dallas Willard wrote in *The Great Omission*, "The first and most basic thing we can and must do is to keep God before our minds... This is the fundamental secret of caring for our souls. Our part in thus practicing the presence of God is to direct and redirect our minds constantly to Him."[10]

But Willard knew that this abiding and redirection of the mind does not happen immediately. This, too, is a "muscle" that must be developed. He went on to say:

> In the early time of our practicing, we may well be challenged by our burdensome habits of dwelling on things less than God. But these are habits—not the law of gravity—and can be broken. A new, grace-filled habit will replace the former ones as we take intentional steps toward keeping God before us. Soon our minds will return to God as the needle of a compass constantly returns to the north... If God is the great longing of our souls, He will become the polestar of our inward beings.

We have hope that continual prayer is possible! We believe it was a reality for Jesus, Paul, and past saints like Brother Lawrence—and is a reality for our interviewees from around the world. Practicing the presence can become a reality for us as well, and the praying leaders we learned from proposed two steps that work together like two legs walking with God: plans and prompts.

Plans: Arrange the Day Around Prayer

Of the leaders we interviewed, Zehra received the most death threats by far.[11]

Her conversion to Christianity and subsequent commitment to

sharing the Gospel with others in a Muslim-majority context have made her a target, but practicing the presence of God under this threat of death gives Zehra a dependence on the Spirit and closeness with Jesus that is beautiful to behold.

Her ministry is focused on sharing the Gospel through radio and the internet; through her work she's not only led many Muslims to faith in Jesus but also empowered Muslim women in her community in unprecedented ways. Zehra and her ministry partners are seeing miracles reminiscent of those described in the book of Acts: People have been healed and delivered from demonic forces, prisoners have been freed by hyenas gnawing through ropes, and individuals who cannot read were able to read the Scriptures. As she shares the Gospel with unreached people groups, many listeners tell Zehra that they have seen or heard of Jesus in dreams; through her ministry, Zehra is able to bring confirmation and context to those dreams.

Zehra grew up as a Muslim and pursued her faith with "religious zeal." Though her life changed dramatically with her conversion, some practices of Islam—particularly the frequent calls to prayer—have proven useful in pursuing greater intimacy with Jesus. She says, "Now, I don't have a ritual, but I do have a routine. I don't *have* to pray five times a day, but I'm always speaking to Jesus, and I carry my prayer closet during the day. It's completely based on freedom and love."[12]

Zehra has learned the importance of arranging her moments and days around God. "I wake up around four or five in the morning. I roll down from the bed to the floor. I go prostrate and call Him by name and say, 'You are the Lord of my day. You are my CEO.'"

Zehra makes God her first thought, and *every two hours* she takes a ten-minute break to recenter her thoughts on Jesus, closing her eyes and entering into His presence.

Prompts: Ringing Reminders to Pray

The traditional function of a town's central bell tower was to encourage residents to practice the presence of God. In AD 604 Pope Sabinian officially sanctioned the ringing of church bells to announce times of daily prayer.[13] For centuries, bell towers sat in the center of towns across the world, ringing to remind believers to lift their hearts to the Father multiple times per day, ringing out the reminder of God's love and presence hour by hour. "Every hour I need thee" was not just a poetic hymn: It was a concrete reality built into the center of towns throughout the Christian world.

Those who practice the presence of God have learned to build "bell towers" in the center of their daily life. Certain tasks, moments, people, and even landmarks serve as "bells" throughout their day to prompt them to stop and pray, lift up a praise, or whisper a prayer to the God of heaven.

In the prayer lives of the leaders we interviewed there were many different kinds of bells prompting these leaders to return to Jesus, but some of the more common prompts were meals, meetings, moods, and moments.

Meals

In the same way that Jesus looked up to heaven and prayed at meals, all the leaders with whom we spoke use meals as a prayer prompt.

Meetings

We've seen many ministries that pray before meetings. This is quite common. But our interviewees tended to also pray during meetings, pausing to listen to God when they lacked clarity or needed wisdom. Mark Zhou, who is the second-generation leader of a major church planting movement in China, said:

> When we start a meeting, it's so natural. You start with prayer. As the meeting progresses, we'll say, "Let's pause a little bit to experience another perspective. Let's pray in the middle of meetings and see if the Lord's given the favor to do [the thing you're discussing]." People will experience that and say, "There's definitely a change."[14]

The reason for integrating prayer during meetings is clear: The Spirit exists, the Spirit speaks in ways we can understand, and God has insight into the situations addressed in our meetings that we do not. For Mark and many other praying leaders, it would be unsettling and unusual to *not* address the smartest, wisest One in the room.

Moods

Feeling a big or deep emotion is a prayer prompt, both for praying leaders and in Scripture. Here's a partial list of the moods that Scripture identifies as prayer prompts:

- In trouble (James 5:13)
- Happy (James 5:13)
- Sick (James 5:14)
- Stuck in sin (James 5:16)
- Concerned about politics (1 Timothy 2:1–2)
- Anxious (Philippians 4:6-7)
- Mistreated (Luke 6:28)
- Facing persecution (Matthew 5:44)
- Unsure what to say (Romans 8:26)

Mark Zhou acknowledged that it isn't just good things that should prompt us to prayer:

I learned that part of our prayer is to talk to God about our disappointment. *Lord, why? Lord, I put my trust in You.* But then, through brokenness, I learn a new perspective. God brings us into alignment with Him.

The apostle Paul makes a similar point in Philippians 4:6 when he says, "In *every situation*, by prayer and petition, with thanksgiving, present your requests to God" (emphasis added).

Prayer and petition. Why did Paul use two words here? In Greek, the word for "petition" is what we often think of as "prayer": asking for things. When we run through our "prayer list," those are petitions. The other word here is actually the more common Greek word for prayer, *proseuchomai*, which has two parts: *Prós* means exchange. It's a marketplace word, like trading money for chickens. The second part, *euxomai*, means "to wish." Prayer is an *exchange of wishes*.[15]

We hear it in Jesus' prayer in the Garden of Gethsemane: "Not my will, but yours be done" (Luke 22:42). *God, here's what I want, but what do You want?*

The most common word for "pray" in the New Testament isn't about prayer lists and endless requests. The truer, deeper concept is "trade my wishes for God's wishes." Regardless of our mood or how we might be feeling, we are invited to exchange wishes with God in prayer.

Moments

A prompt that has deeply affected me (Ryan) personally is merely seeing strangers in crowds. When I'm in a line, I'll pray for those in front of and behind me. In an airport, I'll pray for whoever is around me. I'll pray silently for my Uber driver. I'll pray for people around me on the street. And sometimes I'll practice just listening to see if the Holy Spirit shares with me something specific to pray for these strangers.

Commuting, waiting in line, and walking down the street are all opportunities to pray for others. Sometimes I'm deeply moved to love those around me, but most times it helps change my mood from annoyed to a bit less annoyed and more loving...and more connected to Jesus.

Leaders use particular moments to prompt themselves to pray: like hiring a new team member or making a major financial decision. One leader shared, "I wouldn't make any decision without prayer. When in a meeting, I ask God to guide me. When you're doing the right thing, your heart is light, not heavy and slimy."

Another leader, when writing his task list, begins each line with "BILJ," as a reminder that everything he does is "Because I Love Jesus."

One leader of a Canadian petrochemical company explains that he's praying on a minute-to-minute basis. " 'Father, what do You think? Father, what do You want?' That sensitivity to the Spirit is so central for me."

Staying in tune with the Spirit is often not about doing different things but just doing them *with God*. Brother Lawrence wrote that becoming more like God "did not depend upon changing our works, but in doing that for God's sake, which we commonly do for our own."[16]

One-Sentence Prayers

One of the most famous examples of the power of a few brief words comes from the Hemingway Challenge. Ernest Hemingway, the groundbreaking twentieth-century author, was known for packing intense meaning into tight, punchy language. According to literary legend, Hemingway once bragged to a group of fellow authors that he could write a story in just six words. They reflexively balked. Then Hemingway uttered the words: "Baby shoes. For sale. Never used." The group was awed by this six-word story that evoked incredible emotion.

If a six-word story can pack such power, imagine the power of a similarly brief prayer. One-sentence prayers help us practice the presence of God amid busy days, in the middle of meetings, or absolutely anywhere we find ourselves. Brief prayers may seem trivial, but research and practice show that a single sentence can reorient our mind, will, and emotions, pointing them back to Jesus.[17]

The leader Nehemiah offers a biblical example of a one-sentence prayer. He was far from his Jewish homeland, working as cupbearer to the Persian king, when word reached him that Jerusalem's walls had been broken down and its gates burned, leaving his cherished city defenseless. He wrote that he "quickly prayed to the God of heaven" in the seconds before answering an important question posed by the king (Nehemiah 2:4 NET). We imagine this wasn't the time for verbosity, yet the prayer was noteworthy to Nehemiah, and out of that moment with God flowed the conviction and courage Nehemiah needed to make a bold request to return to and restore the city.

Again and again, Jesus Himself changed lives and history through a single sentence:

- "Father, forgive them" (Luke 23:34).
- "Father...not my will, but yours" (Luke 22:42).
- "Lazarus, come out!" (John 11:43)
- "Be healed!" (Luke 5:13 NLT)
- "Come out of him!" (Luke 4:35)
- "Little girl...get up!" (Mark 5:41)

One-sentence prayers drawn from a deeply rooted relationship with God carry the power and grace of heaven.

Talking to Him Throughout the Day

As we slow our pace, arrange our plans around God, and respond to prompts, we become people who practice God's presence.

Mark Zhou learned to practice God's presence from his grandma. "She had a posture that, no matter what happened outside, the quietness was there. She was talking to Someone I didn't know. She just sat there listening and smiling and murmuring." As an adult, Mark has put into practice his own version of murmuring, using simple phrases. The two he utters most commonly are "Maranatha [O Lord, come!], Lord, have mercy on me" and "Direct my steps."

Mark and other leaders who have learned to abide in God and practice the presence of God realize that He is near. Some say that "Our Father in heaven" puts the wrong image in our minds because it sounds distant. But "heaven" is more like "in the air," and the air is all around us.

Our Father in heaven isn't *there*. He's here. So near. He's present and waiting for us to turn toward Him.

PRAYER

You are holy, Lord, the only God,
and Your deeds are wonderful.
You are strong.
You are great.
You are the Most High.
You are Almighty.
You, Holy Father, are King of heaven and earth.
You are Three and One, Lord God, all Good.
You are Good, all Good, supreme Good,
Lord God, living and true.
You are love. You are wisdom.
You are humility. You are endurance.
You are rest. You are peace.
You are joy and gladness.
You are justice and moderation.
You are all our riches, and You suffice for us.
You are beauty.
You are gentleness.
You are our protector.
You are our guardian and defender.
You are our courage. You are our haven and our hope.
You are our faith, our great consolation.
You are our eternal life, Great and Wonderful Lord,
God Almighty, Merciful Savior.

—St. Francis of Assisi

PRAYER TOOL

ONE-SENTENCE PRAYERS

Lord, fill my soul with Your peace.

Father, fill my heart with Your love.

Holy Spirit, fill me with Your joy.

Teach me to listen to Your voice today.

Help me understand Your will.

Open my eyes to see You.

Protect my mind, soul, and spirit this moment.

God, You are my God; earnestly I seek You.

Why so downcast, my soul?

Give me Your wisdom in this moment.

Remind me You are here right now.

You are my best thought both day and night.

Make my life a prayer to You.

Hide me in the shadow of Your wings.

Make me a blessing to everyone here.

Show me Your heart.

Help me love everyone in this room.

Help everyone in this room find salvation.

I give You this burden.

Lift my eyes to see You, Jesus.

Forgive my wandering thoughts.

Father, I need You right now.

Take this sin from my heart.

Yahweh, show me Your glory.

Come near, Lord Jesus.

Help me do what pleases You today.

Come bring salvation to the nations.

Come to my neighborhood/family/work.

Remind me of Your love in this moment.
Lord, what do You want?
Show me how deep and long and wide and high Your love is.
Help me be still and not miss Your presence in this moment.
God be gracious to us and bless us, and cause Your face to shine upon us.

_____

CHAPTER 4

LEADERS KNEEL BEFORE THE LORD

I have been driven many times upon my knees by the overwhelming conviction that I had nowhere else to go.

—attributed to Abraham Lincoln

Justin Whitmel Earley's success landed him in the hospital.

In his mid-twenties, Justin was building a family and a career as a corporate lawyer. This was the life he dreamed of: except he was exhausted, overcommitted, and overwhelmed. Eventually his body forced him to slow down when he was admitted to the hospital to recover from exhaustion. When Justin was discharged, his doctor gave him a bottle of sleeping pills and told him to take it easy.

Gladly accepting the doctor's prescription but disregarding his advice, Justin entered the darkest phase of his life—marked by mood swings, hallucinogenic nightmares, and suicidal thoughts—all while garnering praise from his law firm for his achievements. He found "rest" in alcohol and sleeping pills, but he recognized the impact of his growing addictions on those he loved.

Desperation led him to redesign his life.

Justin sketched out his own Rule of Life: a series of daily and weekly habits designed to help him find freedom and rest for his soul; rediscover physical, emotional, and spiritual health; and grow his love for God and neighbor. He recognized the power of habits to shape a person over time, and he hoped his new commitments would bring peace.

The first practice Justin embraced was prayer. Serving on the mission field in Shanghai, China, after finishing college, Justin had met many who described themselves as people of prayer, but he recognized that hadn't been true of *him*. "I talked more *about* prayer than I ever talked in prayer," he says. "It took crisis for me to change that."[1]

As he sought to become a person of prayer, he faced some challenges. "One thing I began to notice was that my mind, probably like everybody else's, is very slippery. It always wants to move in a million directions, particularly when I need to pray the most, because those are the times when I'm either tired, depressed, anxious, scared, or thinking about a million things. I started at some point to realize that if I had a physical marker of prayer, if I was able to get the attention of my body, then I was much more likely to get the attention of my mind."

Kneeling became Justin's physical marker.

As soon as he got out of bed each morning, he knelt on the floor. "As I kneeled, my sleepy mind was shocked into a new kind of moment. It wondered what was going on. What are we doing down here on the cold floor?"[2] At night, he repeated the practice, and at midday, when circumstances didn't always permit kneeling, Justin prayed with his hands open and upturned.

For Justin, cultivating a life of prayer began by constructing "a physical trellis of prayer" through these simple postural changes. "The neat thing about building this trellis of kneeling prayer was that all kinds of other prayer began to grow on it," Justin says.[3] Now, prayer punctuates his days, and he finds his prayer habit has grown.

Justin kneels by his bed in the morning, prays at the door with his sons before school, stops to open his hands in midday prayer, lights a candle in prayer at dinnertime, blesses his sons in prayer at bedtime, and kneels again to end his day. It wasn't a big leap, he says, but rather "little habits that have aggregated over time that when you say them all out loud you think, 'Huh! Maybe I am a person of prayer now.'"

Pray Like Daddy

Rolling out of bed onto my knees was one of the very first prayer practices I (Ryan) tried on a journey to develop my own rhythms of prayer.

It started with just a few moments of prayer. Then I started walking through several psalms on my knees. Then I heard a phrase that challenged me even more.

Matt Chandler, pastor of the Village Church and president of the church-planting network Acts 29, challenges people to pray every morning until their soul is happy in God—then they won't look for happiness in other things throughout the day, like other people's opinions, influence, comparison, success, or detrimental things.

My morning time of kneeling prayer has grown longer still as I drop to my knees until my soul rises to heaven.

There is extensive scientific research on connecting two habits together, or "habit stacking." Studies have found that when two habits are practiced together, one will often cue the body and mind for the other. The act of getting on my knees triggers my mind and soul to take a posture of prayer.

One day, while I was on my knees next to my bed, I sensed someone next to me. I looked over to see my six-year-old son. He looked at me and said, "I want to pray on my knees, too, like my daddy." I'll admit I lost it. Tears ran down my face as my son prayed on his knees right next to me. He's maintained this habit for the past several years.

As we conducted interviews for this book, I was personally challenged to take this habit of kneeling to the evening. Morning and evening kneeling have become anchors for my prayer life, and few other prayer practices have affected me more.

Rediscovering an Ancient Posture

Though Justin and I both experienced kneeling as a breakthrough revolution in our prayer lives, the practice is not new. Scripture is full of examples linking physical posture to heart posture in prayer. Psalm 95:6 invites, "Come, let us bow down in worship, let us kneel before the Lord our Maker."

After King Darius issued a decree that no one was to pray to any other God, Daniel knew the precarious situation he was in, yet three times daily he "got down on his knees and prayed, giving thanks to his God, just as he had done before" (Daniel 6:10).

It's also the posture of Jairus, the synagogue official, when he knows that Jesus is his last and only hope for his beloved daughter. He knelt before Jesus (Matthew 9:18), saying, "My little daughter is dying. Please come and put your hands on her so that she will be healed and live" (Mark 5:23).

Kneeling evidences desperation, humility, and submission.

Although Jewish leaders typically opened their arms and swayed back and forth in prayer, the apostle Paul went to his knees as he prayed for the people and churches he oversaw. "For this reason I kneel before the Father" (Ephesians 3:14).

James, the brother of Jesus, likely author of the book of James, was known as a man of prayer. His habit of kneeling earned him the nickname "old camel knees."[4]

According to Hegesippus, a second-century writer, quoted by Eusebius, the "Father of Church History," "[James] was in the habit of entering the temple alone, and was often found upon his bended knees, and interceding for the forgiveness of the people; so that his knees became as hard as camel's [*sic*], in consequence of his habitual supplication and kneeling before God."

E. M. Bounds, a late-nineteenth-century pastor, summarized, "Daniel kneeled three times a day in prayer. Solomon kneeled in prayer at the dedication of the temple. Our Lord in Gethsemane prostrated himself in that memorable season of praying just before his betrayal. Where there is earnest and faithful praying the body always takes on the form most suited to the state of the soul at the time. The body, that far, joins the soul in praying."[5]

The Heart Posture

There's nothing extra spiritual about praying on our knees. Jesus is abundantly clear that it's all about the heart. In the Sermon on the Mount, Jesus emphasizes the heart posture of prayer:

And when you pray, do not be like the hypocrites, for they love to pray standing in the synagogues and on the street corners to be seen by others. Truly I tell you, they have received their reward in full. But when you pray, go into your room, close the door and pray to your Father, who is unseen. Then your Father, who sees what is done in secret, will reward you. (Matthew 6:5–6)

Although it is our heart rather than our body that must bow, a physical posture can reinforce a spiritual perspective. As Pope Emeritus Benedict XVI said, "When kneeling becomes merely external, a merely physical act, it becomes meaningless. On the other hand, when someone tries to take worship back into the purely spiritual realm and refuses to give it embodied form, the act of worship evaporates... That is why bending the knee before the presence of the living God is something we cannot abandon."[6]

The great lie for leaders is the illusion of our self-sufficiency. We can act as if we have sufficient intelligence and knowledge to solve the problems we face and lead our families, churches, or organizations in our own strength. But it's hard to be arrogant on our knees, where our hearts are reminded that we are first followers, not leaders.

A Kneeling Heart

John Ortberg is one of the most sought-after voices in the world of spiritual formation. He is a hero to many in how he has leaned into spiritual disciplines as an author, pastor, and leader. So when we asked him to describe his personal prayer habits, we were surprised by one of his answers:

"Sometimes I try to pray like an addict."[7]

Why would such an accomplished and internationally respected leader look to prayers from Alcoholics Anonymous?

Alcoholics have already come to a point of realizing their desperate need for God, and as John explained, there is a humility in realizing our need for God.

John went on to share the power of understanding that we are all addicts in some sense. We are addicted to our own desires and have a hard time serving others. We are addicted to busyness and cannot make space for prayer, we are addicted to our pride and our status, and we are addicted to attention and recognition, or any number of seemingly small habits that are not healthy for us.

John described the power of coming to our Father in heaven with both humility and desperation. It's when we humbly recognize our desperate need for God that we find healing, wholeness, strength, courage, and wisdom.

To remind himself of his desperation, John uses written prayers from the twelve-step program. His prayer posture echoes the type of prayer Jesus lauded when He told the story of a man who humbly came before God, beat his chest and prayed, "God, have mercy on me, a sinner" (Luke 18:13).

John is not the only one to conclude that our prayers should flow from desperation. A CFO in Oklahoma and the leaders of a Rwandan bank would agree.

A Leader's Contribution

Don Millican, CFO of Kaiser-Francis Oil Company and formerly the youngest partner at Ernst & Young, one of the largest accounting firms in the world, attended many church committee meetings that opened with a perfunctory prayer before quickly transitioning to what the attendees were going to do for God.

"Doing" resonates with Don. He prefers the concrete to the nebulous. Yet more than a decade ago, God put a question on his heart: "If we really believe in prayer, why don't we spend more time doing it?"[8]

As a "left-brained accountant from a left-brained faith tradition," Don describes himself as an unlikely advocate for prayer, yet "I concluded we were functional deists. We believed God existed, but we didn't really believe He did anything—or at least that He did anything in response to our prayers. Otherwise, we would pray more.

"We certainly pray in times of crisis," he reflects, "but in those cases we can't control the situation, so we resort to our *last* resort: prayer. But when we are in control, in charge, we rely on our own efforts…Prayers for our daily lives, prayers for expansion of the Kingdom, and prayers for protection from the attack of the evil one are not part of our daily rhythm."

Don felt compelled to make prayer his first response, not his last resort.

God also grew in him a conviction that while human efforts might lead to incremental improvements in the church, true breakthroughs would come only as a result of prayer.

This conviction came with a calling. God invited Don to pray over his church's ministry, not just sporadically in the privacy of his own home, but faithfully, on his knees, and in full view of anyone who might pass through the church. "This was about three time zones outside my comfort zone," Don recalls. "I was a CPA and an oil company CFO for goodness' sake!"

He initially resisted, then "capitulated" in August 2017. Monday through Thursday, at nine a.m., Don could be found kneeling in prayer. By the end of the year, he had already witnessed God's work in powerful, undeniable ways.

Still, Don noticed that because of his business background and seniority as an elder, other church leaders often looked to him for decisions during their team meetings. In humility, Don began to recuse himself from the meetings, spending the time in an adjacent room, on his knees in prayer for the team. Despite his extensive skills and experience, Don recognized that his most valuable contribution to the church was his prayers.

"Get Your Mats Out"

Financial institutions have played a pivotal role in Rwanda's recovery from the 1994 genocide against the Tutsi, in which an estimated 10 percent of the population was brutally killed over a span of one hundred days.[9] As the nation began to rebuild, microfinance institutions helped restore trust among community members and brought financial stability to more families. But in 2017, Christine Baingana inherited an unenviable role when she took leadership of Urwego, a microfinance institution designed to provide investments to those typically underserved or unreached by Rwanda's formal financial sector. Despite the bank's noble objectives, it was losing money, facing legal challenges, and confronting low staff morale.[10]

Urwego's leaders created a three-year plan to address these challenges but faced one setback after another. Then COVID hit, and a five-month, country-wide lockdown dramatically impacted all aspects of Urwego's performance and operations. Rwandans were unable to work. "So many people were thrown back into extreme poverty amid this pandemic," Christine lamented. As families were impacted, the organization was, too. Urwego faced massive write-offs as borrowers who could not generate income could not repay their loans. Losses mounted. Challenges escalated. They had run out of ideas. And at this moment of desperation, Christine shares, "That's when the prayer warriors came."

Because financial institutions were essential services, Urwego staff were still permitted to gather at the office. One day, a small group of long-serving staff members came to Christine, declaring, "We have something to say." They were aware of the seemingly insurmountable challenges facing the organization, and in response, they presented a plan for Christine's consideration. They wanted the entire staff to come together for three days of prayer and fasting. Christine agreed.

As the team began praying, they did so on their knees. "We got our mats out," Christine remembers. Kneeling is not the place for casual prayers, and they knew their desperation. Together they spent three days fasting and praying. They prayed over every meeting, decision, and activity, surrendering every action to Him.

As Christine and the team invited God to work in Urwego's day-to-day operations, the impact was dramatic. They felt God's confirmation of the work they were pursuing and His encouragement to press on. Still, the challenges continued as Rwanda reinstated lockdowns. Encouraged and emboldened by the impact of their collective fasting and prayer, the same group of colleagues returned to Christine. "We prayed for three days; we were profitable for five months. How about we pray for a month?"

Beginning in February 2021, a department, branch, or team fasted and prayed each of the twenty-eight days of the month. In July they decided to incorporate praise and thanksgiving, even though they were once again facing lockdowns. Urwego set aside the thirty-one days of August to praise and thank God. Each day, a branch, team, or department led the charge, with Urwego's executive team beginning on the first day of the month and closing on the last day of the month.

Prayer has become Urwego's North Star, and kneeling prayer has become a part of Urwego's story and their regular rhythm of operations. Every February, they have committed to a month of prayer and fasting, followed by a month of thanksgiving each August.

Christine shared, "When we prayed, when we waited upon the Lord, when we listened, God showed us gaps, brought the right people to our team, showed us which products to stop, and which to introduce."

Urwego's turnaround was so significant that Christine was recognized as one of the top ten female bankers in Africa. "The momentum she had led carried [Urwego] through the most challenging operating environments in recent history," wrote *Kenyan Wall Street*.[11] But Christine humbly credits something else: God's faithful response to Urwego's prayers.

"[The turnaround] didn't come out of strategy. God did it, especially during the pandemic. I learned how to be fervent and persistent in prayer and how to trust God," Christine says. "[As a leader], you don't depend on your own understanding. You trust the Lord in all your ways and you depend on Him. I am one of those students of prayer."

Christine and the team she leads at Urwego encountered God in prayer, and the reality of His presence left them longing for more. For Urwego, prayer continues, but also as a member of the HOPE International network, they're making a global impact. The practices and posture of prayer modeled by Christine and the Urwego team have been adopted by other entities and institutions throughout Africa, Asia, Latin America, and Eastern Europe.

Paradoxically, as Urwego staff drew near to the Father in humble dependence, it was falling to their knees that brought the team to their feet.

PRAYER

Jesus, fill my heart with Your love,
fill my soul with Your peace,
fill my mind with Your wisdom,
fill my eyes with Your compassion,
fill my ears with Your voice,
fill my mouth with Your words of life.

May my hands be ever serving You,
may my knees bow in surrender,
may my feet walk in obedience.

Empower me—heart, soul, mind, strength—to live for Your glory,
my Friend and Lord forever.

—Ryan Skoog

PRAYER TOOL

ENGAGING POSTURE IN PRAYER

Here are three ways to incorporate posture into your prayer habit:

1. KNEELING

If you haven't attempted it, try it. Spend the first moments of your day and the last moments of your day on your knees in prayer. Commit for the next seven days.

While on your knees in the morning, try to incorporate a psalm, hymn of praise, or worship accompanied by a time of surrender and humility before God.

In the evening, incorporate repentance and gratitude toward God.

2. HANDS DOWNWARD, HANDS UPWARD

One of the more powerful posture prayers we encountered was a simple prayer of releasing and receiving.

It takes only two to five minutes, so it can be done periodically throughout the day.

Hands Downward

Start with your hands facing downward, open toward the ground as a physical symbol of letting go of all the heavy weights you don't need to be carrying. Let go of:

Anxieties	Stress	Guilt
Fears	Worries	Anger
People	Hurt	Emotional Pain

Place all these things in the strong hands of Jesus.

Hands Upward

Then take a moment to flip your hands upward and receive the grace of heaven. Receive:

Mercy	Love	Forgiveness	Beauty
Peace	Grace	Kindness	Truth
Healing	Joy	Blessing	Compassion

Each of these good gifts are freely available to you every time you stop to receive them from Jesus.

3. LIFTED EYES

We also see several Scripture references to people lifting their eyes in prayer. Most notably, Jesus does this often in the gospels.

Our eyes are symbolic of our attention. By lifting our eyes to heaven, we put our attention on God (our Father in heaven) and acknowledge Him with our thoughts and focus.

Lifting our eyes is also an act of humility, as we acknowledge that God is above us and sovereign over us.

———————————————————————————

PART II

HOW LEADERS GROW
IN THEIR PRAYER LIFE

CHAPTER 5

LEADERS PRAY THROUGH TOUGH TIMES

There are many things that can only be seen through eyes that
have cried.

—attributed to St. Oscar Romero

The year 2020 was when I (Ryan) got used to the smell of my carpet.
Night after night, I lay on my face crying out to God to save us.

I've been an entrepreneur in the international travel technology sector
for more than a decade. In the early months of COVID, our industry
was hit even harder than the restaurant industry, as countries banned
international travel. In three weeks' time, my team not only saw sales
plummet from thousands of tickets a day to a single ticket a day but also
had to go back and refund six months' worth of sales. Even though I ran
my companies with no debt and generous cash reserves, we bled through
all of it quickly, and then all of our personal resources as well.

My family lost our entire life's savings in a matter of months. I had to
lay off scores of employees who had been with us since the company was
founded. It was one of the hardest things I have ever done. Our business
loss was so tragic that it made the *Washington Post* as a feature story of
COVID's damage to small businesses.[1]

In addition, my daughter started having nightmares every night. They
were graphic visions of evil spirits coming to her saying they were going
to torture young girls in Nepal we had been praying for. (Our children
pray regularly for the girls our nonprofit, VENTURE, has rescued from
trafficking.)

She would wake up so traumatized that she would run to the bathroom and vomit. Many mornings she pleaded with tears in her eyes, "Daddy, make them stop, make them stop..."

Night after night, I would lay awake on my face in front of her door, crying out to God to spare my daughter, rescue our companies, and save my family from bankruptcy.

There were many nights after a long session of prayer when I felt even more depleted and defeated. I spent hours in prayer, yet things got worse.

After months of fervent prayer, I showed up in the office one Monday morning, crushed by the weight of knowing we could not make Friday's payroll. I was days away from shutting the doors, and my daughter was still waking up every morning in tears.

I broke down and cried before the Lord like no other time in my adult life. Then something life-changing happened.

I closed my eyes and saw a picture of Jesus. And He was crying, too. I saw the tears coming down His face. I heard a voice in my heart say, "Ryan, you've never cried alone; every time you've cried, I've cried with you."

I was instantly overwhelmed with the intense love of Jesus. My tears of pain turned to tears of gratitude for love beyond comprehension.

"Jesus wept" not just at the death of His friend Lazarus (John 11:35). Jesus weeps. He cries alongside everyone who cries. In that moment, I experienced the height, depth, breadth, and width of the love of Christ all at once (Ephesians 3:18). I thought of every time I cried throughout my life and saw Jesus sitting there with me, crying with me out of His infinite love. Then I thought of everyone who has ever cried and of Jesus crying with them, too. This Jesus who "lives to intercede" for us is crying with us, praying for us, and suffering with us (Hebrews 7:25).

I cannot describe it any other way, but I felt His love come over my heart, soul, mind, and, yes, even my physical body. I don't have better words. Analogies sound trite. But His love was not just in my heart at that moment; it engulfed me.

Two days later, my wife and I felt compelled to pray with our daughter and take communion with her; for the first night in three months, she did not have a nightmare. We took communion the next night, and it was two straight nightmare-free nights. So began a new part of our family Rule of Life, where we take communion every night with rare exceptions. I bought a wholesale box of communion cups—the kind that churches typically purchase—and night after night, our family makes a small dent in the inventory.

My encounter with Jesus changed everything.

I understood, perhaps for the first time, why Job was content in not receiving an answer to his seemingly unjust suffering and the great question, "Why?"

God shows Himself, and Job closes his mouth and worships (Job 40:4–5, 42:5). An encounter with God is better than an answer to our questions.

After my encounter with the love of Jesus, I was not consumed or even bothered by the "why" question. Like C. S. Lewis, I could say, "I know now, Lord, why you utter no answer. You are yourself the answer. Before your face, questions die away. What other answer would suffice?"[2]

As long as Jesus is close, it doesn't matter quite so much. As the psalmist wrote, "When I tried to understand all this, it troubled me deeply till I entered the sanctuary of God" (Psalm 73:16–17).

A few days after that experience, our company secured financing to carry us through the season of lockdowns, and we survived. But I am more grateful for that encounter and closeness with Jesus than the rescue itself.

It sounds crazy, but when I look at the pain of that period and the closeness of Jesus in that moment, I can say with confidence, "Worth it."

The closeness of Jesus is worth the painful season if we immerse ourselves in Jesus in these perilous moments. Immersion in the love of Christ is truly beautiful and far beyond any business success.

Splash-Overs of Heaven

Joni Eareckson Tada, founder of Joni and Friends—an outreach to thousands of families affected by disability around the world—knows suffering. A diving accident broke Joni's neck at the age of seventeen, and she has lived with quadriplegia and chronic pain for more than fifty-five years.

"For the longest time I tried to twist God's arm so He'd reveal *why* I had my accident," she shares. "I was banging on the doors of heaven, demanding an answer to prayer, a reason for my horrible plight. I was insistent, almost belligerent, with God. All the haggling didn't quiet my anxieties or soothe my fears in the middle of the night when I was alone."[3]

Much like I (Ryan) did, Joni found the gift of God's presence in her suffering. When all is going well, it's easy to become complacent in prayer and forget our reliance on Christ. But pain invites us to wake up from our self-centered slumber and experience Christ's divine presence and nearness.

"During those lonely midnight hours I didn't feel so cocky and arrogant in front of God," Joni says. "At those times I pictured Jesus visiting me." These visions of Christ with her in her pain grew Joni's trust and humbled her as she realized, "The same God who ladled out seas, carved out rivers, pushed up mountain ranges, and dreamed up time and space cared enough to console me."

After three years of depression and suicidal despair following the accident, Joni says she prayed "the most powerful prayer" of her life: "God, if I can't die, show me how to live, please!"[4]

In His sovereignty, God taught Joni to live mindful of her need for Him. And even though her pain continues, she counts it a blessing. "If you were talking to me without this disability, I don't know what I would be telling you about prayer," she shared. "It's my quadriplegia: God bless it," she said without a hint of irony.[5] There was nothing glib or flippant in her words. Her gratitude amid suffering made it undeniable that Joni has experienced Christ's presence in her life through her pain. She believed her words and found a way to help us believe them, too.

"The prerequisite for earnest prayer, the kind of prayer that storms the gates of heaven, is neediness. You have to know your need for the Lord Jesus," she says. For Joni, disability is a constant reminder of her need, but for most leaders this can be a challenge. Joni speaks of the temptation for Christian leaders to rely on their own resources rather than calling upon heaven. "Usually they rise to Christian leadership because they're good leaders. That is such a built-in danger," she says. "They're the ones who really have to be on guard."

Tough times remind us of our need and invite us to turn to Jesus, just as Joni says the rhythms of her day and the pains that keep her awake at night prompt her to talk with God.

Throughout the night, Joni's husband, friends, or hired nurses turn her body in bed to prevent pressure sores and to relieve pain. These "watches of the night" often turn into impromptu three a.m. prayer meetings. She encourages her nurses—even those who don't yet know Jesus—to memorize Scripture with her, and in the moments when Joni is in great pain and can scarcely find the words to pray, she speaks God's language back to Him, defaulting to memorized Scriptures, stanzas of favorite hymns, or prayers from the Book of Common Prayer. "My prayers are shaped by the Word of God and great suffering," she concluded.

Joni offers a prescription for praying through tough times that counters most of our common practice. When facing a need, she spends 20 percent of her time in prayer addressing the need itself—asking for deliverance or a change in her circumstances—and 80 percent asking God to grant her "courage in it, patience in it, endurance in it." Through prayer, she asks, "What can I learn about Christ from this? How will God reveal Himself to me through this?"

In 2010, Joni was diagnosed with stage three breast cancer, and after five years, she was declared cancer-free. But in 2018, the cancer returned. Joni shares that the van in which she and her husband, Ken, travel to work or to medical appointments is "a sanctuary of prayer," and she remembers one particularly moving discussion in their sanctuary. "As my husband was driving me home in the van from chemotherapy one day, we were talking about how suffering is like little splash-overs of hell...waking us up out of our spiritual slumber. And we pulled in the driveway, and he said, 'Then what do you think splash-overs of heaven are? Are they those easy-breezy bright times, where everything's going your way? Where you have health?' And we said, 'No. Splash-overs of heaven are finding Jesus in your splash-over of hell.' And to find Jesus in your hell is ecstasy beyond compare."[6]

In the Valley

The gift of struggle, valleys, dark times, pressure, and pain is closeness. It's presence. The closeness of Christ can redeem the worst times and the hardest struggles.

David hid this truth in his much-loved Psalm 23. A casual read can miss this subtlest of changes that changes everything.

The psalm starts out by describing God in the third person. "*The Lord* is my shepherd . . . *He* makes me lie down . . . *he* refreshes my soul."

But then something changes.

David moves from the third person *the Lord* to referencing God in the second person, *You.* There is a marked change in the closeness.

When does this happen?

It happens in the valley of the shadow of death. "Even though I walk through the darkest valley, I will fear no evil, for *you* are with me" (Psalm 23:4, emphasis added).

It's in the valley when our relationship with God changes from *the Lord* to *You.*

A friend walked with his mother through a prolonged fight with cancer. She pressed into her relationship with Jesus during this time and felt a closeness she had never experienced before in her life. After winning her battle against cancer, she said she almost missed the struggle because of the closeness. She went from *the Lord* to *You* in the valley, and it changed her forever.

This is why Jesus says, "*Blessed* are those who mourn" (Matthew 5:4): because the comfort we receive is the closeness of Christ.

Sometimes God answers with miracles, but many times His answer is a moment in His presence. Either way, Jesus hears and answers when we seek Him in tough times.

Praying through the Night

Jesus said, "My soul is overwhelmed with sorrow to the point of death. Stay here and keep watch with me" (Matthew 26:38). He, too, prayed through the night amid His deepest grief and agony.

His commitment was to suffer with God in prayer rather than avoid suffering and be out of God's will. And in that moment of suffering, in the garden called Gethsemane, which means "oil press," His soul was pressed and the oil of healing for the nations came out.

His honesty in prayer in front of His closest friends was more brutal than any public prayer we've heard a leader pray.

Father, I'm weak.

Father, I don't want to fulfill the very purpose of my life.

Father, I don't want to go through the very task I came to Earth to accomplish.

Father, can we do this a different way without all this suffering?

... Nevertheless, I will do it.

Jesus wrestled and prayed through imminent betrayal, abandonment, physical torture, fatigue, and slanderous, false accusations. These weighed upon Him to the point that He sweated blood in prayer (Luke 22:44).

This is the prayer that Jesus invited His disciples to hear and participate in. He wanted His disciples to know this: If God in the flesh felt this way on Earth, certainly we will, too.

As Christ mourned, He was blessed with the comfort of angels. He was strengthened to face torture, death, and even hell itself through an encounter with His Father.

The leaders we interviewed around the world—from scientists and business titans to saints, mystics, and missionaries—had been marked by real, powerful, unexplainable, miraculous experiences with God in prayer. Most often, these encounters did not occur on the mountaintops but in the deepest and darkest valleys.

Terry Looper founded a company that at its peak generated $6 billion in sales.[7] That's the GDP of the entire country of Belize. But Terry's story includes valleys as well as peaks, and in a time of anguish and anxiety, Terry encountered what he calls "the love of Jesus."

After achieving his first major business success at age thirty, Terry experienced severe burnout. He was stuck in his bed, unable to move and unsure if this new reality of physical, emotional, and spiritual debilitation might be permanent.[8]

After lying in a dark room for several hours, thoughts swirling, Terry crawled to his knees and pleaded with God to take control. After that anguished prayer of surrender, Terry says, "My brain did flicker on again. But it was only a flicker." Terry's recovery and rediscovery of God as not only Creator and Ruler of the universe but also Lord of his life spanned many months.

Roughly a year after that most difficult day, Terry was simply resting and praying one morning when he encountered the love of Jesus. "I felt myself being embraced by an overwhelming warmth and tenderness," he says. "There was so much affection and acceptance in it, I couldn't stop crying. I knew that Jesus was with me." His encounter with Jesus was so real it changed him, not just in the moment but enduringly. It made him "more loving and more lovable" as a leader, husband, and father.[9]

Terry does something unique to remember his experience. Twice annually he takes a two-day retreat to get alone with Jesus and, in a sense, "re-create" that moment. He reminds himself of that encounter and reimagines it, keeping it always before him.

Over time, the pain of the past can fade, but so, too, can the beauty of God's consolation if we don't make an effort to remember. That's why the Jews marked and remembered encounters using altars, mementos, pilgrimages, ceremonial dinners, and times of reflection. It's why Rosebell keeps a ledger of answered prayers and encounters with Jesus (Chapter 1).

During the tough times we need to remind ourselves of the encounters we have had with God.

When praying leaders face major challenges, they remember their past encounters with Jesus. This becomes the pathway to joy, even in suffering.

Joy, Our Act of Defiance

Ganesh[10] serves in Nepal in the shadow of Mount Everest, planting churches with VENTURE and rescuing girls from trafficking. Many times the rescued girls become church planters themselves. His work is so effective that in several cities so many came to Jesus that the brothels shut down for lack of customers.

But another leader, jealous of Ganesh's ministry, paid a few girls to publicly accuse him of abuse. Ganesh's name was in the national news as an abuser. Following the accusation, donations dried up, cutting off funds that sustained and trained more than 700 rescued girls.

On top of this stress, Ganesh was hit with another crisis. Maoist soldiers started threatening and torturing his staff. They tortured Ganesh at gunpoint and shot one of his staff in their church offices.

The unjust allegations and deadly persecution were devastating attacks. Compounded with the normal stresses of leading a ministry, the pressure became so great that Ganesh started having heart problems. (This was all happening around the same time that my (Ryan's) daughter was having nightmares about Nepal.)

Ganesh followed Jesus' example and went to a mountain to pray for a couple of days. In these focused, intense days of prayer, God gave Ganesh something he calls "defiant joy." It seems impossible to have joy in a moment like the one Ganesh experienced, but he had such assurance of God's provision and redemption that he felt defiant joy well up in his soul. "Joy," Ganesh says with a spark in his eyes, "is a Christian's act of defiance in the face of tough times."[11]

As investigators looked into the accusations, Ganesh's name was cleared. The girls confessed to being paid to falsely accuse him, and the leader who slandered his name wrote a public apology, recanting the false accusations; the national paper reported on his innocence. Ganesh was even given an award for his service to vulnerable children, and the public recognition opened doors to lobby his government on behalf of low-caste and trafficked children. As a result, the government granted land rights to a low caste for the first time in 300 years.

That experience in prayer marked a turning point in his life.

Now Ganesh goes to the mountain monthly for a day of prayer. He also built a separate shack on his land to have a room to go and pray every morning for at least an hour. He needed the separate room because Ganesh is inspired by praying loudly. "Remember to regularly pray LOUD," he advises. "Your soul needs to hear you praying loud every once in a while. I think God likes it too!" This echoes King David, who wrote in his distress, "Hear my *loud* cry, my King, my God" (Psalm 5:2 MP1650, emphasis added).

In his morning prayer in his room, Ganesh prays for his leadership teams, his family, his ministry, and his own heart. Each finger on his hand stands for an individual or a group for whom he prays. As the nearest finger to his heart, Ganesh's thumb reminds him to pray for those he holds dear. Moving through his hand, Ganesh's index finger reminds him to pray for teachers and leaders because of the power they exercise. He associates his middle finger, because of its height, with those who have a platform (actors, writers, "influencers," etc.). As a weaker finger, the ring finger reminds Ganesh to pray for those who are ill or vulnerable. Lastly, his smallest finger reminds him to pray for himself and his own leadership. Ganesh trains his leaders to do the same thing.

And since starting his prayer room, the church-planting movement Ganesh launched with VENTURE has planted more than 4,000 churches in unreached areas and among Nepali communities in fifteen countries.

Praying through this toughest season has resulted in miraculous grace and fruitfulness.

Stay Enchanted with Jesus

We heard an interview with a leader who witnessed firsthand the unraveling of a well-known ministry. Unlike many of his former colleagues, this interviewee wasn't jaded or bitter about the experience, and he seemed to radiate the love of Christ, even after seeing the worst of Christian leadership up close. The interviewer could not help but notice and went off-script to ask this leader why he had fared differently than so many others.

This leader's answer could be summed up in one pivotal insight for Christian leaders: *Stay enchanted with Jesus.*

He credited enchantment with Jesus for keeping him from an endless cycle of deconstruction and cynicism and helping him fall in love with Jesus all over again.[12]

Staying enchanted with Jesus carries us through darkness, stress, and pressure with otherworldly joy.

Tough times, pernicious people, broken relationships, and unexplained tragedies are poisons trying to deaden our enchantment with Jesus. These times require us to dig deeper into our prayer times and cry out like Jacob, "I will not let you go unless you bless me" (Genesis 32:26).

Praying one's soul happy in the darkest valleys is an act of true defiance. It shouts to the world, *The eternal love of God is greater than my current pain, and I will not stop seeking God until "the things of earth . . . grow strangely dim in the light of His glory and grace."*[13]

When facing a crisis, praying leaders don't grit it out; they pray it out.

PRAYER

I arise today
Through God's strength to pilot me;
God's might to uphold me,
God's wisdom to guide me,
God's eye to look before me,
God's ear to hear me,
God's word to speak for me,
God's hand to guard me,
God's way to lie before me,
God's shield to protect me,
God's hosts to save me
From snares of the devil,
From temptations of vices,
From everyone who desires me ill,
Afar and anear,
Alone or in a multitude.

Christ with me, Christ before me, Christ behind me,
Christ in me, Christ beneath me, Christ above me,
Christ on my right, Christ on my left,
Christ when I lie down, Christ when I sit down,
Christ in the heart of every man who thinks of me,
Christ in the mouth of every man who speaks of me,
Christ in the eye that sees me,
Christ in the ear that hears me.

I arise today
Through a mighty strength, the invocation of the Trinity,
Through a belief in the Threeness,
Through a confession of the Oneness
Of the Creator of creation.

—St. Patrick (ca. 377)

PRAYER TOOL

PSALMS TO PRAY DURING TOUGH TIMES

Psalm 3: "But you, Lord, are a shield around me, my glory, the One who lifts my head high" (v. 3).

Psalm 13: "How long, Lord? Will you forget me forever? How long will you hide your face from me?" (v. 1)

Psalm 18: "He reached down from on high and took hold of me; he drew me out of deep waters" (v. 16).

Psalm 22: "My God, my God, why have you forsaken me? Why are you so far from saving me?" (v. 1)

Psalm 23: "Even though I walk through the darkest valley, I will fear no evil, for you are with me" (v. 4).

Psalm 27: "The Lord is my light and my salvation—whom shall I fear?" (v. 1)

Psalm 42: "Why, my soul, are you downcast? Why so disturbed within me? Put your hope in God" (v. 5).

Psalm 46: "God is our refuge and strength, an ever-present help in trouble" (v. 1).

Psalm 91: "Whoever dwells in the shelter of the Most High will rest in the shadow of the Almighty" (v. 1).

Psalm 121: "I lift up my eyes to the mountains—where does my help come from?" (v. 1)

Psalm 126: "Those who sow with tears will reap with songs of joy" (v. 5).

Psalm 130: "Out of the depths I cry to you" (v. 1).

CHAPTER 6

LEADERS PRAY SCRIPTURE

Keep this Book of the Law always on your lips.

—Joshua 1:8

With more than 100 million views in more than 200 countries, videos from BibleProject and its cofounder Tim Mackie have become some of the most globally beloved Bible-teaching resources. Bible reading and study come naturally to Tim, a self-described "Bible nerd," but his journey with prayer has been more complicated.

Tim grew accustomed to connecting with God intellectually through Scripture, but he says, "I was woefully weak in connecting my heart to God through prayer."[1] As he sought to love God with all his heart, soul, mind, and strength, Tim went to a spiritual director, who recommended that he simply spend extended time in silence every morning, holding his hands open and inviting God to speak with him. Tim put this idea into practice. "And do you know what happened?" he asked. "Nothing happened. Like, for a very long time, nothing happened."[2]

We, too, have felt this at times. We've listened in prayer and heard nothing but silence. We've spoken and felt as though our words were bouncing off the ceiling, or we've wanted to speak and been unable to find the words. Prayer has sometimes felt boring, one-sided, futile, or, yes, like a waste of time.

But God has spoken and is still speaking through His words in Scripture, and praying Scripture can bring new depth and passion to our prayers. In fact in the Old and New Testaments, we often see Scripture being used as prayers unto God.

In 2 Samuel 7:27, David reminded God what He had revealed to Nathan earlier:

> Lord Almighty, God of Israel, you have revealed this to your servant, saying, "I will build a house for you." So your servant has found courage to pray this prayer to you.

Solomon, in dedicating the temple in 1 Kings 8:29, reminds God of Scripture like this:

> May your eyes be open toward this temple night and day, this place of which you said, "My Name shall be there," so that you will hear the prayer your servant prays toward this place.

Even Jonah, for all his shortcomings, quotes Psalm 103 and Psalm 145 (among other passages), when he prays:

> Isn't this what I said, Lord, when I was still at home? That is what I tried to forestall by fleeing to Tarshish. I knew that you are a gracious and compassionate God, slow to anger and abounding in love, a God who relents from sending calamity. (Jonah 4:2)

Over time Tim developed practices that joined Scripture and prayer together, using the language of the Bible to pray and studying the Bible as an experience of prayer. He found a way to combine his love for biblical study with a passion for prayer, taking his cues from biblical examples, as well as the church fathers and their practices of *Lectio Divina* and imaginative prayer.[3]

Lectio Divina

Lectio Divina (translated "divine reading") entered the daily prayer practices of early monastic communities in the sixth century as a way of communicating with God through Scripture. It is about reading…and rereading…and rereading a short passage of Scripture with the Spirit's presence. Some describe it as "dialoguing with God" through Bible reading.

To practice *Lectio Divina*, we select a passage of Scripture and invite God to speak through it, reading it slowly and out loud. We listen for words or phrases that come to our attention as we read. On rereading, we reflect on different feelings, thoughts, or impressions, as outlined in the prayer tool at the end of this chapter.

The Bible teaches and commands repetition. For example, in Deuteronomy 6:7 (NLT), Moses instructed the Israelites to repeat the Lord's teaching "again and again."

Like Moses, Joshua instructed, "Keep this Book of the Law always on your lips; meditate on it day and night" (Joshua 1:8).

The psalmist pledged, "With my lips I have repeated every regulation that comes from your mouth" (Psalm 119:13 GW).

There is power in steeping in God's Word. Tim Mackie attests that God often reveals the most important things after rereading a passage multiple times.[4]

Imaginative Prayer

Imagination often feels like the realm of children and eccentrics, but the God-given gift of imagination offers fertile ground in which to grow our connection with Jesus. The idea of imaginative prayer dates to Ignatius of Loyola (1491–1556), who championed the power of using imagination when praying or reading Scripture.

Ignatius proposes:

1. Pick a story out of Scripture. Become familiar with the characters, facts, and scenes by reading the passage slowly.
2. Imagine standing right there, watching the story unfold. Ask questions like "Who and what else are there? What noises are in the background? What smells permeate the air? What is the weather like?"

3. Now begin to picture the scene. Who is in it? What conversation takes place? What is the mood: Tense? Joyful? Confused? Angry?

"The Ignatian questions have given me the keys," Tim says. "What are the strong emotions, points of stress, things I'm confused about?" As Tim reflects on the answers to these questions, he talks with God—and he listens. "I also am puzzled by how life works and wonder, 'Am I hearing my own thoughts, or the Holy Spirit?'" But when Scripture comes to mind, it's clear that it must be God talking. "In my experience, Scripture is the main vehicle through which I hear myself addressed by God."

Tim sees even the difficult parts of Scripture as an invitation to prayer. "When we come across hard things to understand, that's not a problem to solve; that's an invitation to unpack mysteries with God," he says.

As Tim has found, Scripture is not only a text to study and apply but also an invitation to enter into new depths of conversation with God.

As Tim continued to invest in his prayer time, he says, "I started noticing things happening at other times throughout the day. My prayer times with my children became rich, even powerful, I started seeing more prayers answered, and eventually, these morning times I started tapping into what I believe Jesus called paradise."[5]

Praying Scripture: A Ladder to Heaven

In Northern Nigeria, Christians are regularly persecuted, kidnapped, and martyred. Islamic militants have seized and destroyed homes and villages, leading to a crisis of widows, orphans, internally displaced persons, and children unable to attend school. Still, Japhet Yanmekaa, leader of a church-planting ministry, proclaims, "Nigeria belongs to Jesus."[6] Amid threats to his life, Japhet prays and immerses himself in Scripture for up to seven hours each day: four in the morning and three at night.

His God-given, Scripture-driven mission comes from Revelation 11:15, which says, "The kingdom of the world has become the kingdom of our Lord and of his Messiah, and he will reign for ever and ever." Japhet describes this verse as "my vision, purpose in living, and—if need be—the cause for which I will die." Japhet is working "to see Christ enthroned over all nations, people, and tongues" and knows this work will "require much prayer, discipleship, partnership, evangelization, and church planting."[7]

Scripture forms the language of his prayers. "When we stand praying, holding the promises in the Word of God," he says, "we are actually standing on the solid rock that cannot fail; God is committed to bringing His words to pass."

Even in describing his prayer life, Japhet punctuated each point with a verse from the Bible. "We need to prioritize prayer as if all depends on it (Luke 18:1, Acts 6:4); and have a place, time, and hours of prayer (Acts 16:13, Acts 3:1); and depend entirely on the Holy Spirit for burden and direction (Romans 8:26–27)..." and so on. Scripture has so shaped his mind that Japhet seems incapable of speaking without citing the Scripture that undergirds the point he's making.

Through his Scripture-fueled life of prayer, God began to use Japhet to unleash miracles almost daily, including healing those who were blind, crippled, deaf, or battling cancer.

As a young Christian in the early 1990s, Japhet had gone out to evangelize. In the first home he entered, a little girl had died and her relatives were assembling to arrange her funeral. Japhet felt God reminding him of His words in Hebrews 11:35, "Women received back their dead, raised to life again," urging him to pray over this young girl.

Romans 8:11 promises that the same power that raised Jesus from the dead lives in us, and Japhet called upon that power to raise the dead to life again. For half an hour, he prayed over the girl with passion and conviction. Nothing happened. Then he remembered Jesus' words in Mark 5:37–43, when He raised Jairus's daughter. Just as Jesus had done when He healed the little girl, Japhet dismissed others from the room. He prayed and prayed and repeated Jesus' words: "Talitha koum!" ("Little girl, I say to you, get up!").

Miraculously, the girl returned to life. "When we pray scripturally, we are reminding God of His promises that are Yes and Amen to the glory of God the Father" (2 Corinthians 1:20), Japhet says.

Japhet recently had the privilege of visiting the girl, who is now a young woman and the mother of a new baby.

"I lack words to appreciate God for answers to prayers. It is He that works in us both to will and to work for His good pleasure," Japhet says, quoting Philippians 2:13 . . . naturally.

Japhet encourages everyone to imitate Jesus in all aspects of life, but especially in their prayer lives, asking Jesus how to pray, just as the disciples did in Luke 11:1.

New Testament authors quote the Old Testament more than 800 times. Jesus Himself quoted the Old Testament seventy-eight times and the "prayer book" of Psalms sixteen times. As He died on the cross, Jesus prayed Scripture, asking the Father first, "Why have you forsaken me?" (Psalm 22:1, referenced in Matthew 27:46) and then proclaiming, "Into your hands I commit my spirit" (Psalm 31:5, referenced in Luke 23:46). To talk with Jesus was to hear Scripture.[8]

To make our prayer life more like Jesus' prayer life, we need to be immersed in Scripture and let its words shape us.

Receiving a Vision of a Scripture-Driven Prayer Life

One obvious motivation for praying Scripture might be that it has the words we lack, but beyond that, praying Scripture ensures that we are praying in line with God's will and helps us to pray prayers that are both strong and specific.

Strong. Japhet says, "Miracles are but a normal Christian experience as we follow the teachings of Jesus. 'And as ye go, preach, saying, The kingdom of heaven is at hand. Heal the sick, cleanse the lepers, raise the dead, cast out devils: freely ye have received, freely give'" (Matthew 10:7–8 KJV).

There is nothing tepid about the way Japhet prays. He encouraged us to make bold requests and pray for miracles.

Specific. Ask, "What would need to happen to show us that it was God who acted?" One leader told us, "Vague prayers get vague answers; specific prayers get specific answers."

In asking God for help in a situation, we can ask Him to help us imagine and pray for the "answer state," in which we will have no doubt as to whether God has acted.

While no leader we talked with made it ritualistic, Scripture formed their vocabulary, and they insisted that Scripture-connected prayer was more fruitful, partially because it gave them confidence and faith that they were praying in alignment with God's will. These "three S's"—strong, specific, and scriptural—have begun to inform our prayer habits.

Praying Scripture in Practice

A decade ago, Alexander McLean, founder of Justice Defenders, a charity active in prison communities across Africa, discovered the practice of *Lectio Divina* from a group of Benedictine monks.

Alexander was actively working and building an organization to address inequities and bring justice to prison systems across Africa, but he realized, "There's power in making time to balance action with contemplation," and so the Justice Defenders team added *Lectio Divina* to their regular weekly routine.[9] They committed to stillness and prayer *as well as* advocacy and action, and Alexander described their times of reflection and listening as "hugely sustaining and life-giving in the midst of work that can be overwhelming."[10]

During the pandemic, when their meetings moved online, the Justice Defenders team began to open these life-giving *Lectio Divina* sessions to others.

They cast a wide net, inviting supporters, government officials, religious leaders, people in prison, and those whose release from prison had already been secured. They've been joined via Zoom by the former Archbishop of Canterbury as well as various Supreme Court justices, welcoming this geographically and situationally diverse group to come before God to study and pray Scripture together.

Praying Scripture has given Alexander a point of access to invite many in. Spiritual depth and wisdom are not correlated with power, wealth, and position—and in prayer, incarcerated people and government officials find themselves on equal footing. When they practice *Lectio Divina* together, people in prison pray for national leaders and, likewise, national leaders pray for incarcerated individuals by name: an experience that is at once humanizing and divine.

Two Paths to Scripture-Filled Prayer

"Praying the Scriptures is so important in the Christian life," says John Piper, founder of Desiring God. "If we don't form the habit of praying the Scriptures, our prayers will almost certainly degenerate into vain repetitions that eventually revolve entirely around our immediate private concerns rather than God's larger purposes."[11] All the leaders we spoke with emphasized the importance of Scripture in prayer. But they took two distinct paths to Scripture-filled prayer.

Some "Bible their prayers" by adding words of memorized or divinely revealed Scripture to their conversation with God, and others "pray their Bibles."

Bible Your Prayers

One approach is to enhance prayers with the words of Scripture. One pastor, for example, has memorized all of Paul's pastoral prayers and uses selections from them to pray for his congregants.

Others take their prayer requests and ask God to reveal Scriptures to them that fit the need, which can help them ensure that they're praying God's will and, in their view, adding power and faith to the prayer.

Pray Your Bible

John Piper practices the second approach: "Pray your Bible." He says, "Put the Bible in front of you and simply read a line and turn it into a prayer. Paraphrase it, expand on it, apply it to yourself and others."[12] When people ask John how to pray longer, he tells them they can pray all day if they're praying Scripture!

John has tried other methods and found them wanting. When he doesn't have the Scriptures in front of him, guiding his prayers, he's found that he battles repetition. From day to day and hour to hour, "I just pray the same things all the time," he says of praying without the Scripture as his guide.[13]

He writes that he also battles distraction. "My mind tends to wander, and I think instead about what I'm wearing, or that there is a venetian blind that is halfway open." But "the Bible holds my attention" and "it gives me biblical things to pray for so that I'm not praying for empty, vague requests like 'God bless them' and 'God bless that.' Rather, I'm asking for specific things."[14]

John went on to give a specific list of recommended passages for this kind of "praying the Bible," including Matthew 5–7, Romans 12, 1 Corinthians 13, Galatians 5–6, Ephesians 4–6, Colossians 3–4, and 1 Thessalonians 5. "You will be surprised how many insights come as you really take Scripture seriously and try to pray it into your life," John said.[15]

John, as well as many of the praying leaders we interviewed, spoke highly of praying the Lord's Prayer and the powerful picture of a relationship in its opening lines:

> The prayer I have probably prayed more often than any other...is "Father, cause your name to be hallowed in my life and through my life"...I can recall during my seminary days ending my morning jogging in Pasadena by sprinting east on Orange Grove Boulevard as the sun was coming up, and praying with my arms in the air and my heart pounding, "God only give me life—only keep my heart beating—if it will cause people to hallow your name. Let your name be hallowed by my life!"[16]

Scripture is filled with powerful prayers—and gives us the words to pray powerfully.

PRAYER

Our Father in heaven,
Hallowed be Your name.
Your kingdom come.
Your will be done
On earth as it is in heaven.
Give us this day our daily bread.
And forgive us our debts,
As we forgive our debtors.
And do not lead us into temptation,
But deliver us from the evil one.
For Yours is the kingdom and the power and the glory forever.
Amen.

—Matthew 6:9–13 NKJV

PRAYER TOOL

LECTIO DIVINA

Four Steps *in* Lectio Divina

One method of *Lectio Divina* is to read a passage four times, focusing each reading on one of the four steps outlined by Guigo, a twelfth-century monk who elaborated on the sixth-century practice St. Benedict introduced. Our friend Bill Gaultiere of Soul Shepherding shared his approach to these four steps, perhaps best understood as four underlying rhythms, that are embedded in the process of Scripture meditation.[17]

In Latin, Guigo's divine reading steps are *lectio* (reading), *meditatio* (meditation), *oratio* (prayer), and *contemplatio* (contemplation). In English, you can use four *R*'s to remember the four steps as read, reflect, respond, and rest.

1. Reading

"In *Lectio* to read the word of God is to *take it as food and put it into your mouth*. You listen carefully to Scripture—without hurry or intellectual strain. You wait quietly for the Holy Spirit to bring God's word to life. Then you pause on the portion of the passage that you're drawn to."

2. Reflecting

"To meditate on Scripture is like *chewing your food*. You reflect and ponder its deep meaning. Gently repeat to yourself a phrase from the Scripture, turning it over and over in your thoughts and feelings to renew your mind (Romans 12:2)."

3. Responding

"Praying Scripture is like *tasting your food*. You respond to the words with feelings, confess your sins or struggles, and ask God for what you or others need."

4. Resting

"To contemplate on God's word is to *digest its sweetness*. You rest quietly in God's loving arms. No words are necessary at this point and may detract from simply being in God's loving presence. This is the goal of *Lectio Divina*.

"Some spiritual teachers add a fifth step in *Lectio Divina* of *incarnatio*, which is incarnating the Word by living it out in your daily life."

Three Questions in Lectio Divina

1. One Word

What is one word or phrase the Holy Spirit impresses on you? In silence, meditate on that.

2. Feelings

What do you feel? What specific situation in your life today relates? Write down a prayer or pray quietly.

3. Invitation

What is God's personal invitation to you from the Scripture? You can write down what the Lord may be saying to you or a prayer of thanks. Or simply rest quietly in the Spirit's presence.

How to Pray in Lectio Divina

"We have to listen in a very personal and intimate way to the word of God as it comes to us through the scriptures," writes Henri Nouwen, "let[ting] the word descend from our minds into our hearts."[18] *Lectio Divina* is one method for doing this.

After each of the several Scripture readings in *Lectio Divina*, stay in quiet prayer for a few minutes (depending on available time and spiritual readiness).[19]

Here are some biblical passages to approach through *Lectio Divina*.

- Ephesians 1:16–20
- Ephesians 3:16–21
- Philippians 1:9–11
- Colossians 1:9–12
- The Lord's Prayer, Matthew 6:9–13
- The Armor of God, Ephesians 6:10–19
- The Fruit of the Spirit, Galatians 5:22–23
- The Beatitudes, Matthew 5:1–12
- The Ten Commandments, Exodus 20:2–17
- The Great Commission, Matthew 28:18–20
- The Greatest Commandment, Matthew 22:34–40
- Psalm 91
- Psalm 23

CHAPTER 7

LEADERS LEARN TO LISTEN

God speaks in the silence of the heart. Listening is the beginning
of prayer.

—*Mother Teresa*

Andrew van der Bijl sat on the edge of a canal alone one Sunday afternoon in September 1952, lifting his troubled soul to God.

A war injury several years earlier left him with a shattered ankle and
a limp. But in his heart, he heard the voice of God calling him to the
mission field. "Yes, but..." he always answered, naming each disqualifi-
cation and inadequacy. He lacked formal education, and his ankle had
never properly healed. "How could I be a missionary if I couldn't even
walk a city block without pain!" he wondered.[1]

Andrew knew what God was asking him to do, but it seemed
impossible.

Beside the water, he wrestled with God.

Sitting there, he felt compelled to take a physical "step of yes" that
would symbolize his commitment to complete obedience. So he stood up,
and as he went to place pressure on his foot, he felt a violent twist. He
worried that somehow he had hurt his ankle even more. But as he placed
pressure on the foot again, he found that there was no pain or restriction
of movement. He took another step, and then another. His limp was gone,
and he was walking completely normally, just as he had before his injury.

One obedient step, listening to the voice of God, led to a miraculous
healing and then to a life of miraculous steps.

Andrew's first step into missions would be a famous trip that launched a lifetime of sneaking Bibles into communist countries, earning him the nickname "God's Smuggler." His book telling his story sold more than 10 million copies, and his organization, Open Doors, has delivered millions of Bibles and aid to underground Christians in more than seventy countries.

For thousands of years, biblical leaders and Christian heroes have followed this familiar pattern:

- They seek God.
- God speaks and asks for something impossible.
- They take a step of faith in spite of impossibilities.
- A miracle happens.

Jesus Himself had a habit of telling people to do impossible things. To a man who was crippled, Jesus said, "Pick up your mat and walk" (John 5:8). To another individual with a disability, "Get up...and go home" (Matthew 9:6). To a man with a withered hand, He said, "Stretch out your hand" (Matthew 12:13). To a disciple with a few fish, facing the hunger of thousands, He said, "You give them something to eat" (Luke 9:13). To Peter He said, "Come" and walk on water (Matthew 14:29). In each of these examples, the miracle happened when these ordinary people obeyed the impossible word of Christ.

We see this pattern consistently in praying leaders. Their lives were radically transformed through distinct moments of listening and stepping out in seemingly impossible obedience.

Pastors and theologians write and teach about how to hear the voice of God. Some have ten steps and others four steps, but while the number of steps may vary, we found that what matters is:

- a heart that is surrendered to God
- a mind that is fixed on God
- a soul that is quiet before God

Jesus modeled this kind of life, relying on His Father's guidance for His every move: "The Son can do nothing by himself; he can do only what he sees his Father doing" (John 5:19). "The Father loves the Son and shows him all he does" (John 5:20). "Father, I thank you that you have heard me. I knew that you always hear me" (John 11:41–42).

Jesus listened, but we wonder how many of His followers are listening today.

Electric Shock > Silence

Several years ago, a study invited a group of people to spend fifteen minutes alone with their thoughts. The participants were welcomed into a research room and asked to spend the quarter-hour without phones or other external stimuli. They had to remain seated and awake, and the only entertainment on hand was one small button.

Participants were warned that this button, when pressed, would give them a small electric shock. And before the study began, every member of the group had already indicated that they would pay money to avoid a similar shock.

However, the study showed that given the option of sitting in silence or shocking themselves, 67 percent of men and 25 percent of women self-administered the electric shock. "People prefer doing to thinking," the research team concluded, "even if what they are doing is so unpleasant that they would normally pay to avoid it."[2]

The human desire for action is indeed strong, and it impacts our prayer lives.

We'd love to repeat this study with a random sample of leaders, because we surmise the results might be even more dramatic. Many leaders today have become addicted to their own adrenaline (including us). We are accustomed to busyness, to ringing phones, and dinging inboxes. Our days are filled with activity, action, and constant stimuli. We are doers. Would we be among the likeliest to push the button and shock ourselves rather than learn to sit in silence with God?

Prayer is more difficult than an electric shock for many of us.

One leader we spoke with knew the difficulty of prayer, and so each day he started setting a timer for just minutes during which he'd try to listen to the voice of God. When he began, two minutes a day was a struggle. But then it became three and then four, and then longer. Now his timer goes for quite some time every day as he listens in silence before God. He says it generally takes around ten minutes for his soul to quiet down, his mind to stop racing, and the still, quiet voice of God's spirit to be heard.

It takes a concerted effort to develop the muscle of silence. And yet, without making time for silence, we are unlikely to hear from God.

Terry Looper's Sacred Pace

Business titans are not generally the people who come to mind when we think of surrendered prayer lives, but Terry Looper, whom we introduced in Chapter 5, is a friend who has changed our prayers and even the direction of our lives.

Before founding his company in 1989, Terry felt God inviting him to practice what he now calls "sacred pace." God asked him to do something seemingly impossible: Start the company, but work only forty hours a week. If that seemed radical, God's next invitation was even more contrary to the accepted norms and practices of the business world. Terry felt God challenge him to set no sales or growth goals but to simply take care of his employees and his customers and let God grow the business. Since the company's founding more than thirty years ago, Terry has set no metric goals, believing it's far better to commit each decision to God and to wait and listen for guidance.

Terry jokes, "The early church had a plan, but they never set pace goals, they left the pace up to God, and I think they ended up doing okay."[3]

Hearing God is not a single practice for Terry but a way of life. He aims each day to surrender himself to God and die to himself, so he can listen well. He calls this "getting neutral," when he reaches a point of wanting God's will more than his own in any meeting or situation. He surrenders all his daily decisions, even the small ones, because he knows that we first need to learn to hear God in the little things before we can quiet our hearts enough to hear God in the big things.

Every day, every meeting, and every decision is brought before the Lord. Sometimes the conversation is quick and the decision is made, and other times it's a battle dragged out over many prayer times.

Terry gave an example of how he dies to his own desires, enabling him to hear from God in prayer. "This week, I was going to be meeting with a ministry leader who is running his staff too hard, burning them out. I was ready to let him have a piece of my mind. But I make it a point to pray about every meeting I have and ask God what His agenda is for the meeting. I could not hear from God until I died to myself and my agenda. God spoke to me that this leader did not need a reprimand at this point; he needed to be loved. So I died to my agenda for that meeting and listened to God's agenda. By loving this leader, his heart was opened in a new way."

There are stacks of leadership books on how to engage in "active listening." It is a skill that takes practice to acquire in everyday conversation, but if actively listening to a friend or colleague takes practice, then listening to the unseen Spirit of God takes practice as well. Hearing God's voice is a muscle to be developed, and Terry has trained his soul to actively listen to God in the everyday.

Surrender

In our interviews, praying leaders across the globe have a common understanding of hearing the voice of God. Whether they spoke of it or simply modeled it, *surrender* was the key.

Terry explains that when we approach God with our own agenda, our desires are so loud they crowd out the voice of God. They are like the raging wind, quaking earth, and burning fire that the prophet Elijah experienced when seeking God. God's voice could not be heard in any of these things but rather only in a "gentle whisper" (1 Kings 19:11–13). Surrender quiets our desires so we can hear God's whisper.

An Appointment with God

Aila Tasse grew up as a Muslim in a community with no Christians at all, not for miles. When he was in high school, a Christian teacher came to work at the school, and that man shared with Aila the Good News of Jesus. Aila converted to Christianity, and as a result, he was no longer welcome in his family's home. In this time of great upheaval, Aila didn't know what to do.

"I knew that the God of the Bible relates to people differently than Allah," Aila said, "so I thought of Him like a normal person, so I said, 'God, I want to have an appointment with You, and I want You to tell me what You want me to do with my life.'"[4] Aila reasoned, "If He wants me, He should lead me."

Aila set the appointment for ten a.m. the following Wednesday, in the forest.

That Wednesday, Aila bicycled into the forest and arrived at ten a.m. sharp. "I didn't want to be late for the appointment." He laughs. "I treated Him like an invisible human." Aila remembers sitting under a tree, with a Bible, notebook, and a red book called *Sermon Outlines*. "I closed my eyes, and everything around me changed, and I could feel His presence, very heavy around me. I couldn't open my eyes. I'd asked for an appointment, and now He was here."

Aila wasn't sure what to expect next. "I thought that maybe I was going to die," he said. But instead, he saw a vision of his imam, the leader of Aila's mosque. A voice said, "Forgive him and bless him." And so Aila did. Then others who had hurt Aila appeared in the vision. For each one Aila heard, "Forgive them and bless them." And Aila responded in obedience.

"Every time I forgave them and blessed them, something left my heart."

With the work of forgiveness concluded, God gave Aila another vision. He saw a desert he had visited, and a voice asked him, "Can cabbage grow in this place?"

Aila knew that growing cabbage requires a lot of water. Growing it in the desert would be impossible, but as the vision continued, he saw cabbages growing among rocks in the desert.

As the years passed, Aila founded the organization Lifeway Mission International, and he started to share the Gospel across Kenya. God led him to people who began Bible studies, which then led to churches being formed, which led to entire people groups hearing about Jesus.

When Lifeway Mission International began in 1994, there were twenty-six unreached people groups in Kenya; now, largely through the exponentially growing work of Lifeway and its partners, there are just two "and they are being engaged this year," says Aila.[5] Across Eastern Africa, Lifeway is engaged with 146 tribes.

Today, visitors to Lifeway's website sometimes ask about the peculiar logo that adorns its pages—it's a picture of a cabbage, growing in the desert.

Aila's prayer life continued to grow well beyond those initial appointments with God so many years ago. He mentioned three keys to listening in prayer: "There's so much going in our minds, and we are distracted so much," he says, "so you need a quiet place, quiet time, and a quiet heart."[6]

"Your heart will be filled with many things," he says, "and it takes me time, maybe the first five or six minutes, to cool down and settle. Then prayer builds from that. I also check within myself, asking God what's worrying or distracting me. Then I just sing or worship with music and slow down."

While distraction can be natural, Aila knows there are other forces at work when we try to come to God. "I also know that there's spiritual warfare, and the enemy is fighting me," says Aila, "so I start rebuking voices that I'm hearing, or things I'm worried about, or when I haven't yet done something I was supposed to do—assignments that I haven't fulfilled yet—so instead I try to bring those to God. I start confessing things and giving them to God so I can spend my time with God. I can't listen well when my heart is burdened."

One distraction that burdened Aila during prayer was division within his ministry. In a meeting, coworkers had accused him of taking resources from the ministry and wanted him to carve off part of the ministry and give it to them.

"I kept asking, 'God, why did You allow this?' " Aila said. " 'God, You know how honest I am and how I want to serve You. God, You called me, and I am pursuing the call,' but I was not expecting challenges in my life."

Aila then said:

I couldn't even pray. I had a heavy heart and was frustrated and didn't know what to do. I had been in the meeting, and it felt like people were looking for something to accuse me of, like Daniel's adversaries were in Daniel 6. I even lost weight and couldn't eat very well. It was a rainy Wednesday, and I went to pray and was at the back of the church. I couldn't even utter words, but I just wanted to be in the presence of God. I thought, *I can still pray with my spirit.*

On this Wednesday, too, God honored His appointment with Aila. After ten minutes sitting quietly in the church, God broke the silence. "I heard God literally speaking to me," Aila remembered. God said, "The Egyptians you see today you will never see again. The Lord will fight for you; you need only to be still." And then the voice said: "They will come at you from one direction but flee from you in seven." Aila didn't know *which* Scriptures these were, but he knew that these words were from the Bible (Exodus 14:13–14 and Deuteronomy 28:7).

Aila ran to a bus stop, caught a bus, and then ran the rest of the way home through the rain. He burst into his house and told his family, "I have heard the voice of God. The battle is finished."

When Aila next met with his detractors the following week, he sat quietly in the meeting. Aila was amazed to see the word of God fulfilled. "The people who were opposing me started fighting with each other." Their disagreement was so intense that Aila himself had to bring peace *between* two factions of his detractors, and at the conclusion of the meeting, Aila's accusers left by different ways. They never came back.

Get Up and Go

Like Aila, leaders often receive vision and reassurance from God in prayer. They also listen to receive specific direction from God; He frequently tells them to get up and take action.

- "An angel of the Lord said to Philip, 'Go' " (Acts 8:26).
- "The Spirit told Philip, 'Go to that chariot' " (Acts 8:29).
- "And the Lord said to [Ananias], 'Get up and go' " (Acts 9:11 NASB).
- "The Spirit said to [Peter] . . . 'Get up and go'" (Acts 10:19–20).

Something like this happened to me (Ryan) many years ago. It was a Friday night, and I took the night for prayer. I felt compelled to pray for opportunities to share my faith. Right in the middle of the prayer I felt I heard a voice say, "If you want to share your faith, *get up and go* outside your door right now." I wanted to try acting on the impressions I felt in prayer, learning to listen to the little nudges, and so I obeyed.

It was winter, and I was living in an apartment in Sweden. When I walked outside my door, I was promptly hit in the head with a snowball. A bunch of Swedish children were having a snowball fight, and I was a civilian casualty. So I packed some snow and started throwing at their little Swedish coats. It was a blast!

Afterward, the kids asked if they could all come inside for hot chocolate, and while inside one of them saw my guitar and asked if I could teach him. I said sure, and we set up guitar lessons. In a few short weeks the lessons turned into conversations about faith, and through them he gave his life to Jesus.

The *get-up-and-go* voice of God was perfectly, providentially timed.

Later in life, I had a similar experience, just like that Friday night.

It was a Tuesday afternoon in my office. Out of nowhere, I felt an impression so concrete that it was almost as though God had spoken to me audibly. "Get up out of your office right now, and drive over to a local food packing ministry, and ask them for food to send to the war refugees in Myanmar." The command was direct, specific, and immediate.

So I got in my car, drove across town, and showed up unannounced at Feed My Starving Children, a ministry that makes meal kits. I walked in and asked if they wanted to send food to war refugees in Myanmar. Though I had no appointment, I was ushered to one of their top leaders, who told me they had been praying for two years for someone to help them get food to the war refugees. We took a gamble together on the first container, and it made it into the country. We wanted to send more, and through some intervention from the US secretary of state, we eventually built up the infrastructure to serve the region.

Just this year, I'm humbled to write, we celebrated our 55 millionth meal to war refugees. And it all started with simple listening.

Priscilla Shirer and Hearing God

Priscilla Shirer is an internationally beloved author and one of the most sought-after Bible teachers in the world.

She writes and speaks extensively about hearing and obeying the voice of God. A fervent advocate for listening in prayer, she argues that hearing the voice of God "ruins Christianity as usual—once you have sensed the voice of God, you cannot go back to life as you did before." Sometimes the nearness of God and the experience of hearing His voice is more impactful than the specific direction He gives.

Priscilla often teaches that we must match the voice of God with the Word of God. She believes the primary way that God speaks is by illuminating a passage of Scripture, just as Aila described. It might be a passage that comes to mind in prayer, or it might be inviting the Holy Spirit into the Bible reading, giving "a nowness and a newness" to a particular passage of Scripture. It's almost as if that portion "jumps off the page." In these moments, Priscilla believes that God is speaking directly to her.

As a leader, Priscilla has developed a way of talking with God and hearing direction. In addition to inviting God to speak to her through Scripture, she prays for God to give her green, yellow, and red lights.

> *Green light*: This is the "get up and go" command or the experience
> Scripture describes as being "led forth in peace" (Isaiah 55:12).
> *Yellow light*: This is a warning to stay close to the Spirit and press in
> because she's not quite where she should be at the moment.

Red light: This is a clear direction from heaven to stop or run away. (This is the sense my father had when he felt God telling him to run away from the seemingly windfall deal I described in Chapter 1.)

This simple way of communicating with God has helped Priscilla navigate both major decisions and minor ones, bringing each one before the Lord and attending to the light of His direction.

She says that she experiences these lights much like a pilot trying to find the runway to land an airplane: The pilot cannot find the runway with just one light; they need to see a line of lights on the landing strip to know where the runway is and where it is going.

"The bigger the decision that you have to make, the more you need to trust in the mercy of God's external confirmation," Priscilla says. She finds this confirmation in external blessings, provision, and what could otherwise be termed "coincidence"—which she sees as God's sovereign alignment of circumstances.[7]

Listening at Home

As a family, we wanted to give ourselves time to listen to God so we could learn to hear His voice. In our evening prayer times, we spent a couple of minutes in silence just listening, and then we asked our children if they felt like God was speaking to them.

Most nights' listening was uneventful, but some experiences floored us. One night, I was in the middle of navigating a major business decision. A customer had broken an agreement, and I was not sure whether to let it go or pursue the injustice. I was seeking God's direction.

During our evening time of listening in prayer, my daughter felt like she heard the words "Let it go." (This was *before* the blockbuster movie *Frozen* brought those words to the forefront of most American children's minds.) My mind immediately went to the major issue I was facing with our organization; I felt we were supposed to let it go. *God miraculously resolved the situation without conflict.*

Sometimes God speaks to us through others. In that moment, I held back tears from the thought that God would answer my prayer for major organizational direction by speaking to me through my daughter.

Did God Really Say That?

Stories abound of leaders who say "God told me so" to squelch debate, silence dissent, or cover harm. A chapter on listening to God may raise red flags for those who have been harmed by someone who claims to be giving out God's guidance. After all, as author Philip Yancey says, "Not everyone who claims to speak for God actually does."[8]

So how do we discern if we're hearing the voice of God or being swayed by our own impulses? Especially as leaders, the stakes are high if we get this wrong.

Priscilla Shirer has "runway lights," but before there were light bulbs or airplanes, John Wesley had his own tool for confirming God's voice, later named the Wesleyan Quadrilateral. Wesley taught that there are four elements that together help confirm direction:

- Scripture first and foremost
- Christian experience
- Wisdom of Christian tradition through the ages
- Godly reason

The direction we receive in prayer—the impressions and nudges—must be tested against these four authorities, which provide guardrails for us as we listen for God's voice. And even after the direction passes these tests, Scripture gives us another "runway light": our Christian community. As the early church leaders wrote, "It seemed good to the Holy Spirit and to us" (Acts 15:28).

The leaders we interviewed were quick to find confirmation in Scripture, in the leading of the Spirit, tradition, and godly reason, but mainly in community. When leaders received direction or vision—which at times seemed unreasonable or impossible to the natural mind—they humbly took the idea to their community to pray and confirm in their own hearts. This community, of course, must be a safe place for healthy dissent.

God gives direction to leaders, but the vast majority of the time, God gives a hint, the leader brings the hint to a community (whether it is a board, leadership team, accountability group, or close friends), and the community confirms the word from God.

As John English puts it in his book *Spiritual Intimacy and Community*, "There is no individual discernment outside a communal setting and no communal discernment without individual discernment. Each individual profits from the communal activity of discernment and the community profits from each individual's discernment."[9]

We heard story after story of God nudging leaders to pray in specific ways for specific people, God guiding leaders in large and small decisions, and even God warning leaders of danger.

God is speaking.

And Jesus reminds us, "My sheep listen to my voice" (John 10:27).

PRAYER

Lord, grant that I may always allow myself to be guided by You,
always follow Your plans,
and perfectly accomplish Your Holy Will.
Grant that in all things, great and small,
today and all the days of my life,
I may do whatever You require of me.
Help me respond to the slightest prompting of Your Grace,
so that I may be Your trustworthy instrument for Your honor.
May Your Will be done in time and in eternity by me,
in me, and through me. Amen.

—St. Teresa of Avila

PRAYER TOOL

STEPS TO HEARING GOD

Driving humble surrender into the core fabric of our hearts takes work, time, counsel, and flexing a muscle that is sometimes quite underdeveloped. As we seek to listen well, we've found these practical steps from George Müller instructive.

1. I seek at the beginning to get my heart into such a state that it has no will of its own in regard to a given matter. Nine-tenths of the trouble with people generally is just here. Nine-tenths of the difficulties are overcome when our hearts are ready to do the Lord's will, whatever that may be. When one is truly in this state, it is usually but a little way to the knowledge of what His will is.

2. Having done this, I do not leave the result to feeling or a simple impression. If so, I make myself liable to great delusions.

3. I seek the will of the Spirit of God through, or in connection with, the Word of God. The Spirit and the Word must be combined. If I look to the Spirit alone without the Word, I lay myself open to great delusions also. If the Holy Ghost guides us at all, He will do it according to the Scriptures and never contrary to them.

4. Next, I take into account providential circumstances. These often plainly indicate God's will in connection with His Word and Spirit.

5. I ask God in prayer to reveal His will to me aright.

6. Thus, through prayer to God, the study of the Word, and reflection, I come to a deliberate judgment according to the best of my ability and knowledge; and if my mind is thus at peace, and continues so after two or three more petitions, I proceed accordingly. In trivial matters, and in transactions involving the most important issues, I have found this method always effective.[10]

CHAPTER 8

LEADERS REPENT

It is not the absence of sin but the grieving over it which distinguishes the child of God.

—*A. W. Pink*

Pastor Jamie Rasmussen was at the top of his game as a leader, and at the same time, dying on the inside.

His church, Scottsdale Bible Church, was one of the largest and fastest-growing in America. They were seeing people come to Jesus, serving the community, planting multiple campuses, and raising millions of dollars for missionary work and local community service.

But Jamie's schedule and pace had taken a toll on his prayer life. "It's crazy to think that one can run a church and dry up spiritually," he said, but that's exactly what was happening.

He was burnt out. Not just tired but burnt out to the point that he was losing his relationship with the Lord, even as he was teaching the Bible to thousands every week.

Ironically, Pastor Jamie started his ministry as a counseling pastor at Willow Creek Community Church, where he counseled people whose lives, leadership, faith, or marriage had broken down.

Now, at the pinnacle of his leadership, *his* life was following a similar trajectory, and *he* was the one broken down.

We can imagine a host of tragic endings to Jamie's story: turning away from faith as well as ministry, suffering a nervous breakdown, seeking escape in infidelity or addictions, harming his witness and ministry through angry outbursts.

But...

Jamie averted those familiar outcomes. Instead he told his elders what was going on inside him and explained how he was beyond burnt out. He had the humility to recognize that his daily schedule was like a ticking time bomb in his soul.

Wisely, the board came back to Jamie with a surprising mandate: "You need to spend more time with God." Jamie was to block time to spend in prayer and study of the Scriptures, reserving the first two hours of each day on his calendar with the designation, "This time is for God." Jamie obeyed. He cleared his schedule, started a new rhythm, and spent extended time with the Lord.

As Jamie opens his Bible and invites God to speak, he finds that he's changing. "I'm not preparing a sermon, not giving a talk, not doing anything ministry-wise. I'm communing with my Savior. I'm communing with God, and I can tell you this: It recharges my batteries. I end up having a good conversation with Him. I feel more peace...I feel more at rest. I'm becoming more the man He wants me to be...I'm more confident. I feel more free. I'm changing. I got hope."[1]

Jamie's story is not an anomaly. Burnout and temptation are twin threats working together to turn success into failure for leaders around the world.

Vulnerabilities

Throughout the process of writing this book, we had the privilege of learning from incredible praying leaders. But sometimes in our research and conversations, we discovered a lack of intentionality or dedication to prayer where we expected to find consistent and robust prayer.

Of the Christian leaders we spoke with, not everyone who had built a platform had also built a vibrant prayer life.

If identifying well-known leaders with vibrant prayer lives was the first challenge for our project, then the second challenge was that many Christian leaders—both historic and modern-day—have fallen into moral failure. In fact, we debated which sins of commission or omission should disqualify leaders from inclusion in the book, and we solemnly considered what might happen if one of the leaders we've included went on to have a significant moral failing. Or heaven forbid (literally), what if one of us has a similar fall? Should we include a giant disclaimer in the opening chapter?

Jesus drew a connection between prayer and falling when He said, "Watch and pray, lest you enter into temptation" (Matthew 26:41 NKJV). The wording is significant; it did not say watch and pray so that you will not be tempted. Temptation is assumed. Jesus said watch and pray so that when we are tempted, we don't "enter." There is a sense that watchful, prayerful living empowers us to resist temptation when the moment comes.

In Psalm 19:12, David writes, "But who can discern their own errors? Forgive my hidden faults." His words make a strong case for candor from trusted friends—for inviting other followers of Christ to help make us aware of our own blind spots. Many leaders have few trusted friends to inflict "wounds" that just might help them avoid self-sabotage (Proverbs 27:6).

But David's words also speak to our need to directly petition God to remove the blinders from our eyes and allow us to see clearly the sin in our own hearts. Yet how often do we make time and space in our prayer lives to allow the Holy Spirit to bring conviction, which might just lead to repentance and help us avoid making a mess of things?

David invites this scrutiny when he prays, "Search me, O God, and know my heart...Point out anything in me that offends you, and lead me along the path of everlasting life" (Psalm 139:23–24 NLT).

In one instance, God answered David's prayer by sending the prophet Nathan. Nathan used a story to help David see his own need for repentance after David committed adultery and murder. Nathan boldly told King David the story of a rich man who owned vast flocks and herds and a poor man with a single, beloved ewe. When a traveler came to visit the rich man, instead of sharing a sheep from his abundant flocks, the rich man offered hospitality by slaughtering the poor man's treasured sheep. David was incensed. Who would do such a thing? And Nathan had the unenviable job of telling him, *You would* (2 Samuel 12).

Now aware of his sin, David's response is instructive. He penned Psalm 51, a prayer of repentance:

Create in me a pure heart, O God,
  and renew a steadfast spirit within me.
Do not cast me from your presence
  or take your Holy Spirit from me.
Restore to me the joy of your salvation
  and grant me a willing spirit, to sustain me.

Then I will teach transgressors your ways,
  so that sinners will turn back to you. (vv. 10–13)

As leaders who are still prone to blind spots and temptation, we continue to learn from David's example.

A Prayer Life Stops a Denominational Split

Pastor Rob Ketterling was months away from launching a full-scale denominational split.

Rob founded and leads River Valley Church, one of the largest churches in one of the largest denominations in America (Assemblies of God). His church gives almost $10 million to missions every year, making it one of the largest mission-resourcing churches in Christian history.

But Rob had grown frustrated with his denomination. His frustrations spilled out publicly, and as a result he started building a coalition of pastors ready to follow his lead. He wanted to take a few thousand pastors with him and start a variant of the Assemblies of God, splitting the denomination. He even procured lawyers to begin creating the new charter. In his heart, Rob *felt* that he was doing the right thing, taking a bold, courageous step in serving God for the good of the Kingdom. At the same time, as he formalized his plans, Rob sensed a nagging unease.

Rob was faithfully committed to prayer, and part of his Rule of Life was to do the *Examen*. During this extended prayer time, Rob listened for any way he was displeasing God, and in a powerful encounter with God, Rob heard God's voice say to him, "You are going to divide my people and at the same time say that I am behind it?!" Later in this same intense time of prayer, Rob sensed the voice of God again: "If you do this, I will remove my favor upon you, and you will be on your own."[2] The encounter was so real, powerful, and serious that Rob was filled with the fear of God.

He repented of his divisiveness.

Rob called a meeting with the leader of his denomination and confessed what he had been planning. He asked for forgiveness and said he was not only willing to faithfully serve the vision of the denomination but also to publicly confess in front of the leaders of the denomination at their General Council meeting.

Months later, with thousands of national and international leaders watching, Rob humbly confessed the sin of divisiveness and publicly endorsed the denomination, its leadership, and its mission.

Unbeknownst to Rob, an international leader in the Assemblies of God denomination had also been planning a schism in his own country. He was so moved by witnessing Rob's repentance and confession that he, too, halted his plans for a split and sought restoration.

Rob's dynamic prayer life, in essence, stopped catastrophic division and organizational collapse. Had Rob not spent extraordinary time in prayer, we would be reading about the great schism of the Assemblies of God.

As Rob's story illustrates, repentance is not just a nice addition to our prayer life; it is core to our walk with God.

Room for Repentance

I (Cameron) have had the privilege of leading Christians in dozens of countries in training focused on the biblical message of generosity.

In 2019, a group of leaders of various sports ministries across Africa gathered in a hotel for the training. Participants looked at Scripture together, watched video testimonials of radically generous Christians, and shared about their own personal experiences with generosity and giving.

The training began energetically. But partway through the first day of the two-day training, the atmosphere morphed from energetic to mildly responsive to dead quiet. I continued with the training, posing a question related to the material they were studying, and a man named Jean[3] stood up in the back of the room. "I need to stop us and say something," Jean said. Everyone turned around and looked at him.

"I thought I was coming to generosity training to learn how to raise money from people. But it turns out that generosity is first about God's generosity to me. This training is about *me* and *my heart*. And I haven't been generous. I have read the Bible many times, but I have just missed this whole part about being generous. I've expected others to be generous to me. And I need to repent."

Jean suggested they pause the training and take time to repent, right then and there. The group agreed. They cleared the rows of chairs, creating a circle in which leaders knelt, facing outward, and repented, some quietly in their hearts, some with their voices, some reading Scriptures on generosity followed by Scriptures on God's forgiveness.

The group never finished the training, but following this act of public repentance, they have spread the message of biblical generosity to many hundreds of sports teams and coaches across Africa.

The *Examen*

Public repentance, as modeled by these African leaders, can be a powerful practice. So, too, can private repentance—just between God and a leader. The *Examen* (a Spanish term that shares a Latin root with our English word for examination or test) is the name of an ancient practice of inviting God to examine our hearts and lead us to repentance. There are countless versions of the *Examen*, but its essence and origin date back to St. Ignatius in the sixteenth century.

Before he was a saint, Ignatius of Loyola (1491–1556) was a soldier. After being wounded in battle, Ignatius asked to read stories of chivalry to pass the time convalescing. Instead he was given a book of stories about the life of Christ and the lives of the saints. From his reading,

Ignatius converted to Christianity, and when he had sufficiently recovered he journeyed to a place of pilgrimage in northeastern Spain. There, he spent three days confessing a lifetime of sins.

In the days before writing his now-famous *Spiritual Exercises*, in which the *Examen* is included, Ignatius was spending seven hours a day in prayer. As he retreated from the world to draw near to God, he developed the spiritual practice of the *Examen*, which shaped him and remains a pillar of the religious order he went on to found: the Jesuits. Firmly convinced of the *Examen*'s importance, Ignatius required the Jesuits to practice it twice a day: at noon and at day's end.

The general outline and goal of the *Examen* have remained unchanged for centuries, and the practice still impacts leaders today. "The specific exercise of *Examen* is ultimately aimed at developing a heart with a discerning vision to be active not only for one or two quarter-hour periods in a day but continually," wrote Jesuit Father George Aschenbrenner.[4] Out of this dedicated time of examination flows an increased awareness of God's presence and a greater realization of our own need for repentance. The five steps below come directly from Ignatius, and we expound on these in the prayer tool at the end of this chapter.

1. Give thanks to God our Lord for the favors received.
2. Ask for grace to know my sins and to rid myself of them.
3. Demand an account of my soul from the time of rising up to the present examination. I should go over one hour after another, one period after another. The thoughts should be examined first, then the words, and finally, the deeds.
4. Ask pardon of God our Lord for my faults.
5. Resolve to amend with the grace of God. Close with an Our Father.[5]

Antidote to Arrogance

Most leaders are prone to a dangerous combination of natural ability, drive, and arrogance, inflating our egos like ever-expanding balloons.

But if our pride is a balloon, then prayers of repentance let the air out. It's humbling to confess that we've messed up or even hurt people. Doing so cuts away the root of pride and arrogance plaguing Christian leaders and turning people away from the Gospel.

Prayer is often hard work because it's humbling work.

One of the more powerful biblical images of a praying leader is Moses before the burning bush: a leader receiving a vision in the fiery presence of God. The unique requirement for Moses to be in the presence of God was that he had to remove his sandals (Exodus 3:5). Many Jewish scholars believe that sandals symbolized identification, family rights, and land rights, signifying status and possessions.[6]

To walk the hallowed ground, to draw near the fire of God's presence, Moses had to lay down his status. Accomplished leaders often have a hard time doing this, but it's necessary if we want to be close to our God, who promises to be "near to those whose hearts are humble" (Psalm 34:18 GW) and far from the proud (James 4:6).

The praying leaders we encountered throughout our search learned the secret of humbling themselves daily before God. They developed the habit of "removing their sandals" of influence, position, possessions, status, fame, and accomplishments as they bowed in prayer, producing a humble life of leadership and a discernible closeness with God.

PRAYER

God and Father of our Lord
and Savior Jesus Christ,
the glorious Lord,
the blessed essence,
the God and Sovereign of all,
who is blessed to all eternity,
Sanctify also, O Lord, our souls, and bodies, and spirits,
and touch our understandings, and search our consciences,
and cast out from us every evil imagination,
every impure feeling,
every base desire,
every unbecoming thought,
all envy, and vanity, and hypocrisy,
all lying, all deceit, every worldly affection,
all covetousness, all vainglory,
all indifference, all vice, all passion,
all anger, all malice, all blasphemy,
And every motion of the flesh and spirit
that is not in accordance with Thy holy will:
and count us worthy, O loving Lord, with boldness,
without condemnation, in a pure heart,
with a contrite spirit, with unshamed face,
with sanctified lips, to dare to call upon Thee,
the holy God,
Father in heaven. Amen.

—Liturgy of St. James

PRAYER TOOL

EXAMEN

We encourage you to try the *Examen* or another practice of daily repentance.

1. "Give thanks to God our Lord for the favors received."

   We may thank God for the joy of knowing Him, the undeserved gift of His love, or His sacrifice in taking our punishment on the cross.

2. "Ask for grace to know my sins and to rid myself of them."

   We now seek illumination: asking God to shine a light into our souls so that we may see what He would reveal to us, that we might, as King David wrote, discern our own errors (Psalm 19:12).

3. "Demand an account of my soul from the time of rising up to the present examination. I should go over one hour after another, one period after another. The thoughts should be examined first, then the words, and finally, the deeds."

   We now move on to review both consolation and desolation in our day. Ignatius thought of consolation not merely as a bright spot in the day or something that brought joy but rather as something that was truly good for our souls, leading us toward God. Desolation, in contrast, is not just the feeling of unpleasantness or despair but rather things that diminish our faith, hope, and love.

4. "Ask pardon of God our Lord for my faults."

   In light of what God has revealed, we ask Him how we ought to respond. It is here that He invites us to practice repentance, a humble and sincere expression of remorse for our wrongdoing, which may include sins of commission or omission.

5. "Resolve to amend with the grace of God. Close with an Our Father."[7]

Rather than remaining mired in shame or guilt, we move from repentance to look ahead to the future. We might reflect on how we will respond to similar temptations in the future or ask God to show us how we can more faithfully serve Him in the days to come.

The *Examen* closes in praying the Lord's Prayer, directing our attention back to our Father in heaven.

CHAPTER 9

LEADERS SEEK GOD THROUGH FASTING

Feed prayers on fasting.

—*attributed to Tertullian*

Patrick Johnson was at a crossroads.

He believed his calling was to help American churches become more generous, but in the United States, it's difficult for a generosity-teaching ministry to distinguish itself from the armies of fundraisers and church campaign consultants. "Generosity" is often confused with "fundraising" instead of a fruit of the Spirit.

Lots of American churches wanted to raise money; most didn't want to train people in generosity. And that left Patrick flailing. "I hit a wall and was not in a good place," he says.[1]

Unsure what to do, Patrick knew that he needed to seek God in a more intense way. He reached out to an intercessor in Wichita, Kansas, and together they committed to fasting over the next month, meeting each morning by phone at eight a.m. to pray.

Two weeks into the fast, Patrick says that God gave him a spirit of repentance. God showed Patrick that he'd taken his ministry, Generous Church, in the wrong direction. A financial advisor by training, Patrick began to think, *Maybe I should just go back into business.*

But God also guided Patrick to gather a group of "contenders" to fast and pray for global generosity. He began reaching out to friends by email, asking if they'd be willing to join his prayer and discernment process. "I wanted to go deep, not wide," he recalls. "And God brought seventy-two people to pray."[2]

During this season of fasting and prayer, God gave Patrick a new mandate to focus on the global Church. Despite having no international experience, Patrick began receiving inquiries from leaders of massive international movements and denominations, who told him that they were desperate for the kind of training Generous Church offered. Within the year, Patrick was receiving more invitations than he could manage.

No longer anxiously pitching to skeptical American churches, Patrick developed a new experience called the Generosity Design Lab; it's become so popular that Patrick is now in global demand and has to carefully discern which invitations Generous Church should accept. And the message of God's abundant generosity is flowing around the world. Kids on a soccer team in Egypt chipped in to replace their teammate's broken phone; a Nigerian engineer bought a house to start an orphanage; a Middle Eastern family felt led to sell their wedding rings and give to the poor; a woman in Lagos decided to celebrate her birthday with the marginalized in a "blind camp" rather than having a birthday party with affluent friends; nearly 20,000 Malawians have brought a handful of maize to their churches as a way to give to God in an economy where cash is scarce.

In the two years since Patrick's Generosity Design Labs began, more than 17,000 church leaders from seventy-five countries have been impacted by the cascading ripples of generosity training—and those are just the ones we know about—all flowing from a vision sparked in a season of fasting.

Fasting Fuels Prayer

When we asked praying leaders around the world about their prayer practices, we didn't have specific questions about fasting. But during our interviews, these leaders spontaneously shared their fasting rhythms.

Pastor Japhet, whom we learned about in Chapter 6, explains his rationale for fasting: "Just as the body needs physical food for its growth and development, prayer needs fasting for the same reason." Japhet believes that fasting *fuels* a prayer life. He sometimes fasts as many as forty consecutive days.[3]

For the global Church, long fasts are routine. One church-planting movement that serves in a civil-war-torn nation starts the first seven days of every month fasting until seven p.m. They have seen hundreds of churches planted despite intense persecution.[4]

Fasting Prayer Lights Strategy on Fire

Pavel runs a church-planting movement with more than 20,000 churches in some of the most difficult places on Earth.[5] Churches are springing up and multiplying across Central Asia (Afghanistan, Turkmenistan, etc.) as well as Eastern European and Slavic countries.[6]

Pavel is an imposing figure with a booming voice, but tears come quickly when he's talking about the love of Jesus and the power of the Scriptures.

When we asked Pavel how he built a movement of brave and bold leaders who are eager to plant churches in hostile areas, he immediately started talking about the culture of prayer that his wife helped create. While Pavel himself has a dynamic prayer life—rising early to spend at least one and a half hours in prayer and Bible study—his wife influenced him deeply in practices of intercession, which he then passed on to the leaders he trains and churches he works with.

Pavel said he implemented all kinds of strategies to help the churches plant other churches, but it wasn't until they began intense prayer and fasting that they started seeing explosive growth in frontier regions of the world.

Pavel mapped out what a normal year of prayer and fasting looks like for their leaders, and it starts with twenty-one days of prayer and fasting in January, which ends with a full-day prayer meeting on Zoom, attended by thousands of church planters from countries all over the world.

There Is Always Someone Fasting

Pavel wanted his leadership teams to fast, but he didn't want it to happen only periodically—he wanted fasting to be a part of the culture of his teams. And so he started a fasting calendar, allowing leaders to sign up for different days to fast and ensuring that at least one member of the leadership team is fasting at all times. "Fasting never stops for us!" Pavel said, laughing. "We just take turns."[7]

Many leaders we spoke with have adopted this idea of having someone in their organization always fasting. Some organizations do this for a month, others for a particularly intense season, and still others, like Pavel, have done this year-round.

For Pavel's leaders, fasting created an intensity and fire across their teams, strengthening their hearts to face the constant persecution and fear of prosecution where they serve.

What Were Jesus' Rhythms of Fasting?

Fasting was an assumed practice for Jesus. He said in the Sermon on the Mount: "*When* you fast" (Matthew 6:16, emphasis added). He expected His followers to fast, and He made certain that they would fast after He left.

When we think of Jesus and fasting, the first image that comes to mind is of Him fasting in the wilderness before His test with temptation (Matthew 4:1–11). He fasted of course for forty days, and what this passage shows us is that Jesus' extended fasting not only prepared Him to confront temptation but also to confront evil. Similarly, when Christ came down from the Mount of Transfiguration and was able to drive an evil spirit from a young man whom the disciples were unable to help, Jesus told them that there are types of evil that can be confronted only through "prayer and fasting" (Matthew 17:21 NKJV).

Jesus modeled fasting, and fasting strengthened Him.

Fasting somehow teaches us to flex our "no muscle." It's as if saying no to food, TV, or phones for a season allows us to say no to other, more destructive temptations and evils.

Years ago I (Ryan) saw the power of fasting at work when a friend of mine, who is a great leader, was struggling with a particular sin. After praying together, he felt that this sin's power in his life would be broken through fasting. I joined him for the fast, and at the end, he received the power to overcome this habitual sin. He's continued to incorporate fasting into his Rule of Life and has walked in freedom from this sin for more than a decade.

Our Fasting Forefathers

Church history is full of examples of Christians prioritizing fasting for every believer, but especially for leaders.

A book called *The Didache*, written as early as AD 80, closely linked fasting to following as Christ's disciples. Candidates for baptism were to fast, as were those baptizing them and all others in the community who were able.[8]

St. Basil the Great (329–379) saw fasting as a "safeguard" for the soul, effective in helping repel temptations.[9]

The ancients saw fasting as a source of power as well as a way to resist sin. St. Athanasius the Great (circa 293–373) is said to have taught that "Fasting possesses great power and it works glorious things. To fast is to banquet with angels."

St. John Chrysostom (347–407), agreed, arguing that fasting "enlightens the soul, gives wing to, and makes even the scaling of the mountain with ease. The fast is food for the soul."[10]

St. Isaac the Syrian (died circa 700) said, "If the Law-giver Himself fasted, is it not also necessary for those for whom the law is given to fulfill the fast?"[11]

Early Christians also fasted to:

- lament and commemorate Jesus' death
- observe the liturgical practice of stations of the cross

- respond to persecution
- care for the poor and address community needs[12]

Twice a week, often on Wednesday and Friday, early Christians routinely fasted to commemorate Jesus' betrayal and crucifixion.[13]

In more recent church history, fasting has preceded revival. John Wesley (1703–1791) and his friends fasted in community two days every week. Together, they birthed both the First Great Awakening and the Methodist movement that came from it.

Evangelist Charles Finney (1792–1875) prepared for revivals by organizing teams to pray, fast, and spread the word before he arrived; his work helped ignite the Second Great Awakening.

Smith Wigglesworth (1859–1947) was a healing evangelist. At a tough point in his marriage, he fasted ten days to get his heart right, and afterward he reported that his temper and moodiness left. Each week, he fasted and prayed for fifty souls to be saved on the following Sunday. Usually, it happened.

In 1906, William J. Seymour (1870–1906) was on a ten-day fast when he preached in a little house on Bonnie Brae Street in Los Angeles. While he was preaching on Acts 2, the Holy Spirit moved powerfully, and as a result the meetings began to attract more people. Within the week, they moved to a larger building on Azusa Street, and the Azusa Street Revival was born, helping to spread Pentecostalism around the world.

How Dallas Willard Fasted

The practice of fasting spans history and denominational background. Dallas Willard, known for his books on spiritual disciplines, actively practiced the discipline of fasting by setting aside days for abstaining from food.

"I practice short-term, total abstinence from food very regularly, through the week, and especially if I'm in ministry of some sort," he said. He frequently fasted half days, and about once a year, he practiced a three-day, water-only fast.[14]

While Dallas encourages believers to have "days where you're very intensive about solitude, and silence, and Scripture memorization, and fasting," he offers a word of caution, lest we become legalists:

> One of the signs of a healthy use of disciplines is how you feel when you don't do them. If you feel guilt [when you don't do it], then you need to rethink it. Guilt is not a profitable motivation for the spiritual life.[15]

A gifted philosopher, Dallas posited a more metaphysical view of fasting than most others we interviewed and researched. He believed that the Word of God *is* energy. It's God's words that spoke our world into being. "God speaking is a form of energy that became matter...and matter is energy in a certain form," he wrote.[16]

He therefore believed that fasting "can teach us about the reality of the word of God coming to us and sustaining our bodies without the intermediary of matter."[17] This feeding on God's Word as an energy source, rather than food, helps us make sense of Jesus' cryptic response to His disciples in John 4; when they encouraged Jesus to eat, He replied, "I have food to eat that you know nothing about...My food...is to do the will of him who sent me" (John 4:32, 34).

This Forgotten Strength

In a privately commissioned study, the Evangelical Council for Financial Accountability surveyed evangelical leaders and found that a majority of the heads of top-tier Christian organizations aren't fasting. As we've shown, this is an anomaly in Christian history and, frankly, in the global Church. The global Church fasts with regularity, but the Western Church is on the precipice of losing this powerful practice if its leaders don't renew their commitment.

In our interview, Japhet Yanmekaa, whom we featured in Chapter 6, offered some guidance to leaders in the West on rediscovering a passion for fasting and an awareness of its significance—even necessity—in the life of Jesus' followers.

Japhet shared that "a burning vision" fuels his fasting prayer. "Your prayer life will not be consistent without a burning vision," he said, because "a lasting prayer life is oriented around a burden, and every burden comes from a vision."[18] Japhet pointed to Nehemiah 1:3, in which Nehemiah learns that "the wall of Jerusalem is broken down, and its gates have been burned with fire."

When Nehemiah heard this, he sat down and wept. He writes, "For some days I mourned and fasted and prayed before the God of heaven" (Nehemiah 1:4).

Japhet believes that Nehemiah had a burning vision of Jerusalem restored and shared, "A burning vision will make you fast and pray for hours." As leaders, may our God-given vision drive us to fast, and may our fasting feed our prayers.

PRAYER

O God, you are my God;
*   I earnestly search for you.*
My soul thirsts for you;
*   my whole body longs for you*
in this parched and weary land
*   where there is no water.*
I have seen you in your sanctuary
*   and gazed upon your power and glory.*
Your unfailing love is better than life itself;
*   how I praise you!*
I will praise you as long as I live,
*   lifting up my hands to you in prayer.*
You satisfy me more than the richest feast.
*   I will praise you with songs of joy.*

I lie awake thinking of you,
*   meditating on you through the night.*
Because you are my helper,
*   I sing for joy in the shadow of your wings.*
I cling to you;
*   your strong right hand holds me securely.*

—Psalm 63:1–8 NLT

PRAYER TOOL

GUIDE TO FASTING FOR LEADERS

If fasting is new to you, begin by finding a date on your calendar to join these praying leaders in accepting God's invitation to fast. God may have things He wants to say to you or things He wants to do through your ministry that He's eager to reveal when you are so committed to seeking Him that you're willing to give something up in exchange.

These tips for fasting have been adapted from our friend Bill Gaultiere, founder of Soul Shepherding.

- Start small with a short or partial fast. Fasting just one meal each day or completing a partial fast is an effective way to begin experimenting with fasting. Partial fasts include limiting yourself to juices, abstaining from meat, eliminating sugar and junk foods, or eating significantly less than normal.
- Fast from things other than food, like media, shopping, or judging other people.
- Use Scriptures to cultivate your desire for God as you continually turn your thoughts from physical hunger to your deeper hunger for God and His Word. Relate to David in Psalms as he describes the feelings of fasting to portray his desperation for God. See Psalm 42:1–2; 63:1–8; 73:25–26; 119:20, 81; and 143:6.
- Memorize and meditate on Scripture, noticing God's promises. Recommended passages include Matthew 11:28–30, John 1:1–5, Philippians 2:1–11, Colossians 1:15–23, and 1 Peter 2:9–10.
- Intercede for someone in need with concentrated prayer.
- Seek discernment from God about an important decision.
- Talk with a spiritual director.
- Use fasting to learn to rely on Jesus' care for you rather than seeking false comfort from overeating, lusting, reacting in anger, using alcohol, overworking, judging other people, or gossiping.

- Practice relying on the Holy Spirit and not your natural energies and abilities as you minister, preach, serve the hungry (physically or spiritually), or do your work for the glory of God.
- Draw close to Jesus during your fast by meditating on the stations of the cross: steps from Jesus' condemnation to His burial.

CHAPTER 10

LEADERS MAKE SPACE TO RETREAT

You're my place of quiet retreat; I wait for your Word to renew me.
                                                    —*Psalm 119:114 MSG*

Each year, Hala Saad, the leader of Vision Communications International, has a three-day retreat with her prayer partners. The group heads to a cabin in the mountains to pray.

Hala's ministry creates and broadcasts content to share the Gospel across the Arabic-speaking world. Each year, her ministry's work is seen by millions, prompting tens of thousands of calls and social media messages to counselors who are ready to share how inquirers can have a relationship with Jesus.

At the time of Hala's annual retreat a few years ago, Vision Communications was attempting to develop a piece of property in Egypt as part of their expansion strategy. Every phase of the development, from the permitting to the funding and logistics, had been a fight. "All of it felt uneasy. There were tremendous obstacles," Hala recalls.[1]

At first, she thought it was because they were new to developing property and unfamiliar with the process. But then, on their prayer retreat, God revealed to Hala and her prayer partners that the man overseeing the property in Egypt and representing their interests in the development process was actually working against them. He was *creating* the obstacles.

The group prayed for him and, despite his betrayal, blessed him. "We knew this was not God's place for him, so we blessed him and asked God to 'promote' him to a place that's the right fit," Hala says with a laugh.

In Egypt, those with stable caretaking jobs and secure incomes aren't easily dismissed and almost never leave by choice. Hala was afraid that an ugly confrontation would damage her ministry's reputation, so she prayed, "Lord, You have to give me wisdom. I don't feel like I'm supposed to confront him." The group continued to pray for the duration of the retreat.

When they returned from the retreat, the overseer announced that he had found another opportunity outside Hala's ministry and was resigning—effective immediately.

"Sure enough, ever since he left, the development process has accelerated because God undid the obstacles supernaturally," says Hala.

This tremendous breakthrough came not from the ministry team's efforts but from their retreat, as they entreated God to act on their behalf. Just as in fasting we refrain from food to emphasize God's supernatural provision, in retreat we refrain from striving, emphasizing God's sovereignty over our circumstances.

Pace of Prayer versus Pace of Influence

In Chapter 2, we talked about how Jesus went away to the wilderness so often that Luke called Him a slip away and pray-er (see Luke 5:16). Matthew joined in this observation as well. In just three chapters of Matthew, Jesus withdraws or slips away *five* times.

- After He hears about the execution of John the Baptist (14:13)
- After feeding the 5,000 (14:23)
- After a dispute with the Pharisees (15:21)
- After feeding the 4,000 (15:39)
- After the Pharisees and Sadducees demand a sign (16:4)

Regardless of how busy we feel or how much our leadership is valued at work or at home, we cannot dispense with this core practice Jesus demonstrated. As leaders, we can grow addicted to accolades, achievement, or even just the idea of being needed. A profound theme that arose from our research was the way in which prioritizing prayer safeguards leaders against the dangers of chasing influence.

Influence makes a pernicious idol. Leaders can believe they're chasing after God when they're actually chasing their own influence. It's grown to the point that many today define the very essence of leadership as influence. It's largely an American phenomenon, where influence is so closely linked with fame and position.

Influence, like money, is something to steward for God's glory if it comes. But, like money, it's deadly when it becomes an ultimate pursuit.

What's even more deceptive is that we can grow more influential while becoming less prayerful and less Christ-like. In chasing after influence, many leaders neglect families, burn out staff, feed egos for motivation, drive themselves to health issues, pass up genuine needs in search of more influential people, envy and lust after the perks of influence, and even forgo time with God.

Jesus taught His leaders a different priority. Jesus' life on Earth defined leadership as more than influence. He actually said that's the world's definition (Matthew 20:25–28). He often left crowds to pray, sought out the outcast, and passed over influential leaders to invest in uneducated fishermen. Jesus taught His top leaders to prioritize obedience, servanthood, and abiding in Him (Matthew 20:26; John 15:5; Matthew 7:24–29). This combo leads to something better than influence: fruitfulness.

One of the easiest ways to fight the temptation to value influence above God is to lead at the *pace of prayer*. We may be worshiping the idol of influence rather than Jesus if we and those we lead are too busy serving Jesus to have a dynamic prayer life.

Prayerful retreat realigns our priorities, inviting us to renounce our pursuit of influence and renew our pursuit of God.

Retreat invites us to step back from it all to refocus on the One who sustains us. In *Devotional Classics*, Richard Foster writes this about solitude:

Solitude is one of the deepest disciplines of the spiritual life because it crucifies our need for importance and prominence. Everyone— including ourselves at first—will see our solitude as a waste of good time. We are removed from "where the action is." That, of course, is exactly what we need. In silence and solitude God slowly but surely frees us from our egomania. In time we come to see that the really important action occurs in solitude. Only then are we able to enter the hustle and bustle of today's machine civilization with perspective and freedom.[2]

Early Christian leaders applied these principles in a legend about the apostle John. In the legend, John was engaged in the hobby of pigeon rearing. A fellow elder in the church was returning from a hunt with his bow and arrow and teased John for wasting time with his pet birds.

John looked at the hunter's bow, noting that the string was loose. "Why is your bow loose?" he asked.

"I always loosen the string of my bow when it's not in use," said the elder. "If it stayed tight, it would lose its resilience and fail me in the hunt."

John responded, "And I am now relaxing the bow of my mind so that I may be better able to shoot the arrows of divine truth."[3]

It's encouraging that the early Christians—so revered for their diligence and works of mercy—told stories to grant one another permission to relax the bows of their minds.

The Huckleberries Are Everywhere

Tim Mackie, whose practices of praying Scripture are detailed in Chapter 6, speaks of how a retreat became an important time of reframing his own prayer life.[4]

Tim regularly spent time with God primarily through reading and meditating on Scripture, but he often felt feelings of guilt, fear, or resignation about his comparably lackluster prayer life. He didn't desire deeply to spend time with God in prayer. It didn't seem to be a rich experience, and he wondered: Were others experiencing a richness that he was not? Was he simply a Bible person rather than a prayer person?

A spiritual director encouraged him to begin each day in silence, inviting God to speak and reveal Himself in ways that were outside Tim's pattern of engaging with God through Scripture.

After about a year and a half, Tim decided to expand these morning mini-retreats into a three-day time of solitude and prayer, hiking and camping on the north side of Mount Hood in Oregon. The first leg of his journey required a rapid gain in elevation, and so Tim set out determinedly, face to the ground.

About three-quarters of the way to the first fork in the trail, Tim heard rustling in the bushes. He thought an animal was making the sound and became alarmed as he realized it wasn't fleeing. But Tim soon realized the noises came from a woman, crouching in the bushes near the trail. She turned her face toward him, her mouth stuffed full, and gestured to the bushes surrounding them, saying, "Look at these *huckleberries*! They're *everywhere*!"

Tim hadn't noticed. As he was ascending the trail to get to his destination, he had failed to see the huckleberries all around him—this free, beautiful, and abundant provision of God. It isn't just God's provision we can miss on the way to our destination; it's His leading...His movement...His companionship.

During that retreat, Tim realized that he had been shaped by one set of experiences—and they were very good experiences. Hearing from God through Scripture is powerful and life-changing, but it took retreat—stepping away from his usual rhythms and habits—for Tim to experience God in a new way.

Dallas Willard used to say that for transformation to occur, we need "VIM": *vision, intention,* and *means.*[5] Dallas believed that some of us are all about *means*—"What can I *do* to become more like Jesus?"—when our real need may be for clearer *vision* and a renewing of our *intention* to live like Jesus. Dallas saw retreats as especially influential in renewing our *vision*; we think Tim would agree.

For a long time, Tim's understanding of Scripture shaped how he experienced God. But now, for perhaps the first time, Tim's experience of God is shaping how he understands Scripture—and it all began with a practice of retreat.

He's beginning to see the huckleberries, and they're *everywhere*.

How an Aussie Ministry Leader Retreats

In Australia, Richard Beaumont has faithfully led the Entrust Foundation for fifteen years. The foundation supports poverty alleviation and church-planting efforts across Africa and Asia. Over his many years of service, Richard has instilled retreat rhythms into his busy life.

He repeats a quarterly cycle:

- Month 1: Half day
- Month 2: Full day
- Month 3: Two full days and one overnight away from home

Once a year, his wife, Julie, joins him for one of the overnight prayer retreats so that they have time to chat, pray, and plan together. He fixes these dates on his calendar and firmly believes that a fruitful retreat begins before the retreat does.[6]

First, Richard prioritizes the retreat by scheduling it a year in advance and committing to that reserved time. When he has occasionally had to reschedule a retreat, he books it for the next available time. He also begins praying for the retreat in advance. Specifically, he invites the Spirit's presence, asking God for help waiting on Him and acting in the Spirit.

Once Richard has arrived at his place of retreat, he says, "My focus is to stop, listen, slow down, and reflect." He finds it helpful to create a loose structure for the time. While remaining sensitive to the Spirit's prompting, he allots time for prayer walks, reading the Bible or devotional literature, and even napping. He journals what he senses God is saying, whether it's encouragement or ideas to follow up on after the retreat. He avoids screens and also incorporates fasting into his retreat. His recommendations for an effective retreat are included at the end of this chapter.

Silence

Most leaders spend a lot of time talking, but retreat invites us to exercise a different muscle: silence. Sprinkled throughout Richard's, Tim's, Hala's, and even Jesus' practices of retreat is this idea of spending time in silence with the Father.

Author Evelyn Underhill wrote, "*Silence* is at the very heart of retreat...Without silence around us, the inward stillness in which God educates and molds us is impossible...It is an *elected silence*. We cannot find it in the world...Treasure that silence. It will do far more for your souls than anything heard at our services."

Why silence? And why do we need so much of it?

Underhill believes, "Our deepest contacts with God are so gentle because they are all we can bear. We need quiet to experience them. They do not come as an earthquake of mental upheaval or in the scorching fire or rushing wind of emotion. In the silence, there is nothing devastating or sensational, but only a still small voice."[7]

Most leaders we researched needed only one prayer retreat to be fully convinced that this is a necessary part of their life, leadership, and prayer practices. Retreat becomes, in the words of Tim Mackie, a reminder of "paradise" that fuels the rest of their year.

PRAYER

Lord Jesus, let me know myself and know you,
And desire nothing save only you.
Let me hate myself and love you.
Let me do everything for the sake of you.
Let me humble myself and exalt you.
Let me think nothing except you.
Let me die to myself and live in you.
Let me accept whatever happens as from you.

Let me banish self and follow you,
and ever desire to follow you.
Let me fly from myself and take refuge in you,
that I may deserve to be defended by you.
Let me fear for myself, let me fear you,
and let me be among those who are chosen by you.
Let me distrust myself and put my trust in you.

Let me be willing to obey for the sake of you.
Let me cling to nothing save only to you,
and let me be poor because of you.
Look upon me, that I may love you.
Call me that I may see you,
And forever enjoy you.

—St. Augustine

PRAYER TOOL

RICHARD BEAUMONT'S GUIDE TO AN EFFECTIVE PERSONAL RETREAT

1. Go to the retreat location. Then *rest*. Sleep in! Slow down. Enjoy God's gifts. Practice Sabbath.
2. Repent of any sin. Name your sins to God. Name our sins as a church, society, or family.
3. Thankfully review how God has been working. Count your blessings. Celebrate the good things. Thank God!
4. Submit to God's plans for you.
5. Devour the Bible and take notes. Read the Bible slowly; listen carefully and chew on what you receive.
6. Write down specific issues and questions about yourself, your family, and your ministry. Speak about your pains. Make a just complaint. Weep. Wait!
7. Carry the burdens of others to God. Hold others in your heart.
8. Meet with God in a quiet place; take notes.
9. Journal. Respond in writing to questions and issues.
10. Plan how best to communicate thoughts and delegate tasks.

HALA'S SCHEDULE FOR A TEAM RETREAT

Hala says, "Our prayer retreats include a lot of fellowship, fun, and food! This just comes naturally. We always experience a time of being refreshed, sharing, laughing, and bonding. Our gatherings are far from dry and task-oriented."

This is a general overview of the time they spend together.

Day 1, Evening: Reconnect and Catch Up

"The first day is sharing where we are and what God's been speaking over the course of the year." The time isn't just exchanging news. It's focused on spiritual development, reflecting on how God has been moving, both individually and organizationally, over the year.

Day 2, Morning: Worship

The group turns on worship music and sings along, soaking in the presence of God. "Worship is an important part of our three-day retreat," Hala says. "We take our time. We can sit in the presence of the Lord for hours." At some points, Hala will feel led to share some things about how the ministry is doing: organizationally, programmatically, financially, spiritually. Intercessors feed on details and specifics, so Hala understands the importance of details and specifics and aims to give these trusted colleagues the real situations, names, and needs.

Day 2, Afternoon: Focused Prayer

With some themes and context in place, the group dives into various aspects of the ministry. They aren't mechanical but rather allow God to lead them. Hala's team may ask questions as they feel led. As the group listens to the Spirit and asks questions of God and one another, the Spirit offers increasing clarity.

Day 3, Morning: Personal Prayer

On the final morning of the retreat, the group turns from ministry-focused prayers to praying for one another.

PART III

HOW LEADERS MULTIPLY PRAYER WITHIN THEIR ORGANIZATIONS

CHAPTER 11

LEADERS CREATE A CULTURE OF PRAYER

Prayer does not fit us for the greater work; prayer is the greater work.

—*Oswald Chambers*

Mark Batterson had a challenge.

As the author of one of the best-selling books on prayer, *The Circle Maker*, Mark believed in the power of prayer. He wanted not only to be a person of prayer but also to create a culture of prayer in his community, church, organization, and leadership teams. But the frantic pace of Washington, DC, was working against him.

As the founder and lead pastor of National Community Church (NCC) in the US capital, Mark leads some of the busiest, most in-demand people in the world. Getting his congregants to slow down and pray presented a challenge.

But Mark's challenge is fundamentally the same as that of any leader who is on the journey from growing in prayer to building a culture of prayer. How does *any* leader translate a personal passion for prayer to a culture of prayer in an organization, community, or leadership team?

That question guided our interviews and study of praying leaders, and these final chapters will unpack their practices and recommendations on creating cultures of prayer.

144 | Leaders Create a Culture of Prayer

Model Before Multiplying

It's no accident that the first ten chapters of this book focus on *personal* practices and postures. We cannot create *cultures* of prayer without first becoming *people* of prayer. We must model before we multiply.

In Acts, when confronted with a critical need requiring wisdom and leadership to restore unity to the growing Church, the twelve disciples delegated this responsibility to men "known to be full of the Spirit and wisdom"—so they could devote their attention "to prayer and the ministry of the word" (Acts 6:3–4). Those most directly responsible for spreading the Gospel and establishing Christianity as a movement considered prayer—not problem-solving—the best and most fruitful use of their time.

As we discussed above, Jesus modeled this dedication to personal prayer. His time was limited, with only three years of formal ministry. Yet He modeled and even explicitly taught prayer (Luke 11), and then He invited others in, creating a culture of prayer. In Luke 18:1, Jesus tells His disciples a parable "to show them that they should always pray and not give up." But this was not a new teaching. This was something they had seen Jesus practice and prioritize over the years they had spent together.

In the practice of the early Church, we see the ripple effect of the culture of prayer Jesus established among His disciples.

When the apostles sought a replacement for Judas after his betrayal and subsequent death, the remaining eleven disciples "all joined together constantly in prayer, along with the women and Mary the mother of Jesus, and with his brothers" (Acts 1:14). Following this intense period of prayer, the Holy Spirit launched the Church on the day of Pentecost (Acts 2).

When Peter was imprisoned, awaiting trial and execution, the Church gathered to pray for him. Acts 12:12 says, "many people had gathered and were praying" when an angel miraculously led Peter out of his jail cell. At the guidance of the Holy Spirit, the early church at Antioch commissioned Barnabas and Saul with fasting and prayer (Acts

13:1–3). Scripture is filled with examples of leaders inviting others to pray not only *for* them but *with* them, to engage together in a culture of prayer.

Lead by Example

Like all the praying leaders who create a culture of prayer, Mark Batterson realized it must flow out of the leader's personal example.

Mark's Rule of Life includes starting each day with Bible reading and a double-shot latte. Mark journals thoughts, prayers, and verses that speak to him: words he believes God is giving him. Then he goes back over his journal and prays over initiatives, words from God, and verses he wrote, turning each highlight in his journal into a moment to pray.

Mark smiled as he talked about how his prayer times can effortlessly drift into hours of communion with Jesus.[1] He practices and enjoys "wasting time" with God regularly. Books, blogs, sermons, dreams, vision, and strategy have all come out of these prayer times.

Building Culture

With his own prayer rhythms firmly established, one of the first things Mark did to ingrain prayer at National Community Church was to "use creativity to create culture."

He called his team and congregation to pray at 7:14 a.m. and 7:14 p.m. every day. It was intentionally 7:14, as a nod to 2 Chronicles 7:14: "If my people, who are called by my name, will humble themselves and pray and seek my face and turn from their wicked ways, then I will hear from heaven, and I will forgive their sin and will heal their land."

He oversaw the construction of a prayer room in their head offices and invited staff to join together for intercessory prayer three times per week. These prayer meetings have become cultural anchor points of National Community Church.

Knowing that leaders staff their most important initiatives, Mark next hired a prayer coordinator. This full-time member of the leadership team coordinated prayer and at times had no formal responsibility other than to pray.

Mark shares that another key to creating a culture of prayer at NCC has been creating a "culture of testimony." Mark grew up in an old-school Pentecostal, Sunday-night-testimony, Tuesday-night-prayer-meeting church culture. He vividly remembers stories of God turning lives around in dramatic answers to prayers.

Remembering the impact of these stories, Mark started a Tuesday night prayer meeting. It is not attended by thousands, but hundreds come regularly. Mark quipped, "Last time I checked, all it took was 120 people in an upper room to usher in Pentecost."

At the Tuesday night prayer meeting, people share stories of how God has answered prayers and how they have experienced His presence in challenging situations. The stories are spread throughout the church community to stir faith to "stop and seek God."

Mark has also instituted a unique prompt to prayer that shapes the organizational culture. He invites his colleagues to pray in conflict. "If someone gets under your skin, they just made your prayer list," he says with a smile. This habit of using feelings of frustration or annoyance as a "bell" prompting prayer has become a beautiful way to get closer to God and others in the same moment, impacting the attitude and tone of the entire organization.

Renewing Organizational Culture Through Prayer

In another bustling East Coast city, Steve Shackelford[2] has seen prayer renew and revive organizational culture. Steve leads Redeemer City to City, a ministry co-founded more than two decades ago by the late pastor Tim Keller. From the beginning of his ministry in New York City, Tim had a heart for church planting and church multiplication, and when leaders in distant global cities began to see what was happening in Manhattan in the early 1990s, they collaboratively extended this vision and mission into cities around the world. Today, City to City has helped pastors and leaders plant almost 1,000 churches and train or impact more than 79,000 leaders in major cities and cultural centers worldwide.

Steve's path to ministry wasn't typical. Before joining City to City in 2017, he worked with the international accounting and auditing firm PwC for ten years, primarily serving the Walt Disney Company and Disneyland Paris. Steve went on to serve as CFO, COO, and president of public real estate investment trusts, then spent the last five years of his corporate career with one of the largest business development companies in the United States. But if the staff of City to City expected to find a particular type of institutional leader in Steve based on his background, they may have been surprised when they got to know their new CEO.

During his first six months on the job, Steve sought to listen and observe. As one might expect of a ministry significantly influenced by Tim Keller, Steve found that City to City was filled with brilliant and erudite thinkers, entrepreneurial pastors, and church planters and staff deeply committed to the mission and vision.

Despite these significant strengths, Steve discerned that the organization was facing some cultural and leadership challenges. At the time, Tim Keller served as chairman of City to City and was still working full-time as lead pastor at Redeemer Presbyterian. The organization, as one consultant quipped to Steve, was a "twenty-year-old start-up." With that designation come beauty and opportunity but also disorganization and chaos that can lead to wounds and disunity.

Over time, Steve began to seek leaders for his senior leadership team whose deeper organizational and managerial skills would help construct a trellis behind the beauty of City to City's entrepreneurial heart.

Ultimately, Steve knew that City to City desired to see a Gospel renewal pour through global cities, and he knew it would not happen without prayer. Steve often quotes John Smed, who wrote in his book *Prayer Revolution*, "Every kingdom movement starts with prayer."

Instituting a culture of prayer in a global organization took some heavy lifting, but Kimberly Hunt, who serves as City to City's chief of staff, and other leaders helped Steve carry the load. Kimberly exemplifies the type of leader Steve wanted at the helm of City to City. In addition to her remarkable managerial skills, Kimberly consistently speaks the Gospel into Steve, encouraging him to start and end his days and meetings with prayer and to build his personal and communal muscles around prayer.

While certainly prayer was not absent within City to City prior to 2017, it seemed like an add-on rather than something central to the lifeblood of the organization—a sidecar rather than a driver. Steve was convinced that God was inviting City to City to become more and more defined by prayer, not just by intelligence, theological breadth, or outcomes. "There is a large prayer element to this work, and it's something that we work hard to inculcate into the work that we do," he says. "That piece of the equation is seminal...It's not going to happen in my view without that."[3]

City to City dedicated a year to reading and discussing *Prayer Revolution* in their staff meetings. During COVID, staff would gather online one morning each week to pray. Departmental prayer began to grow, both intentionally and organically, as leaders began to integrate their prayer practices into their work rhythms. Donors in a few cities even began to gather in prayer monthly for the fundraising work.

Surprising outcomes arose and continue to arise as the teams gather regularly for extended prayer. "An unusual commitment to prayer will lead to unusual results from prayer," Steve says. "In a journal I keep, I've recorded more than forty requests, hopes, or issues where I believe God has miraculously answered as it relates to City to City."

In our discussions with Steve, we were struck by the revelation that before joining City to City, he had been praying for a ministry opportunity like this for *more than twenty years*. Over the course of two decades, God not only prepared Steve with relevant skills but also refined his character and reshaped his beliefs until he had become the praying leader City to City needed for this season. By the time Steve took the helm, he viewed personal achievement as "a spiritual minefield."

Steve couldn't have predicted that he would lead the organization and its staff through a global pandemic and the loss of Tim Keller, their iconic pastor and leader. After six and a half years in the role, Steve somewhat jokingly remarked, "I don't think God delivered this type of opportunity to me at a younger age [Steve is fifty-nine], as I wasn't ready professionally, spiritually, or emotionally. This has been the hardest job I've ever had."

The Lord continues to refine Steve's leadership as he seeks to understand more fully what it means to be a leader of no reputation, as Paul talks about in Philippians 3. What does it mean to operationalize the concept of "giving power away" and "leading out of weakness"? How do we resist the leadership temptation to elevate ourselves, so we are prepared to fight "the need to increase" that becomes the undoing of so many leaders? "The way of Christian leaders is not upward mobility," he says, paraphrasing the late Henri Nouwen, but "downward mobility."

Steve's desire is that City to City will "continue to cultivate and grow a culture of prayer" because he truly believes prayer matters. At the end of our interview, Steve asked a question that poignantly lingered: "Why would you lead out of your own strength when you could tap into the resources of heaven?"

For thousands of years and into the present, praying leaders like Steve have tapped into the resources of heaven.

The Team Takes On the Personality of the Coach

Todd Peterson has one of the more remarkable leadership journeys we encountered. He was a twelve-year NFL placekicker who played most of his career for the Seattle Seahawks (where he was named NFL Man of the Year in 1996), Kansas City Chiefs, and San Francisco 49ers before retiring with the Atlanta Falcons in 2006. Beginning late in his NFL career and continuing through the present, Todd has spurred the acceleration of Bible translation by stewarding his personal generosity and influence to build an international alliance called illumiNations.

This "collective impact alliance" envisions translating at least a portion of Scripture for 100 percent of the world's population, a New Testament for 99.9 percent, and a full Bible for 95 percent by 2033.[4] It's a seemingly impossible vision, given that Bible translators previously projected it would be 2150 or later before they'd enter the last languages. By encouraging collaboration, illumiNations strives to reach the original goal more than one hundred years ahead of schedule.

Not surprisingly, Todd is a praying leader. "When you're attempting something big, you don't blow off prayer!"[5] he told us with the passion of an NFL player. "Every decade that goes by I realize how foolish I've been for not praying more. The longer you walk with God, the more you realize you can't pray too much."

Todd continued, "People have different leadership roles and serve in different contexts, but leaders who pray have humility." Humility fuels a life of prayer and prayer in turn fosters a life of humility. Todd's humility and prayer life have helped him encourage collaboration among eleven multinational nonprofits coordinating Bible translation efforts around the world.

Working under many NFL coaches taught Todd some key lessons about culture-building. "Organizations take on the characteristics of their leader; a team takes on the personality of its coach. Likewise, a culture of prayer can only be created by leaders who don't simply talk about prayer but actually pray. If you tell your team you pray for them and they know you're actually praying for them, that changes everything."

With these insights, Todd and his partners in this alliance have resourced prayer initiatives among Bible translation leaders and other donors. They host calls with participants from all over the world where they pray. "No small talk; we pray," Todd highlighted. During these calls they pray through relevant Scripture and agree in prayer as each participant lifts their biggest challenges up to the Lord.

These prayer meetings have become the foundation of a culture of prayer. And this culture of prayer is fueling illumiNations's mountain-moving goal of making God's Word accessible in every language.

Deep Dependence on God

Florence Muindi spent years in preparation before beginning her work leading in ministry. In 1999 she founded Life in Abundance International, an organization that partners with local churches and leaders to sustainably meet social, economic, educational, and health needs within their communities in fourteen countries throughout Africa and the Caribbean. Since its founding, Life in Abundance has served more than 1 million people with their holistic ministry model.[6]

Though Florence grew up in Kenya, she felt God call her to minister in neighboring Ethiopia. Sixteen years after her "heart was first broken for Ethiopia," Florence finally had the opportunity to travel there to discern a ministry opportunity.[7]

During those sixteen years, the Lord faithfully guided Florence to medical school and specialized training, and then to ministry experiences, equipping her to do the work He called her to do in Ethiopia. Those intervening years deepened her reliance on the Lord, helped her learn to discern His voice, and grew her friendship with Jesus. "I would talk to Him about everything and listen to His guidance," she remembers. "I would go for long walks and invite Him to come along with me. I would speak to Him as if He was human, walking by my side…All this was setting the stage for what was coming…Waiting time is not wasted time."

When she was establishing her ministry in Ethiopia, Florence says intercessory prayer was her first step. Before launching any new initiative, she and local church members would prayerfully walk through the community, "inviting the kingdom of God."

After a few years, ministry seemed to be humming along. Florence had competent leaders in place, the team was growing, and the work was advancing. But Florence recognized the unique threat posed by good times: prayerlessness. When things are going well, "we tend to think we do not need prayer because we are engaged in 'spiritual' things. How wrong we are!" she realized. "It is an irony to be involved in God's work without constantly seeking His guidance. He has the blueprint, yet we go about guessing or trying to figure out what it is He wants us to do for Him. I have very often fought the desire and urge to do things the way I know how, leaning on my own understanding."

As God continued to reveal to Florence more of His vision for Life in Abundance, He was constantly calling her into uncharted waters, deepening her and her team's dependence on Him. "The practice of prayer becomes inevitable as I recognize that I am pursuing something bigger than myself and I do not even know the pathway for a God-sized vision that is impossible to achieve or sustain without His leading and enablement. Prayer becomes a true felt need."

From its earliest days, Life in Abundance implemented an overnight prayer session the last Friday of every month, as well as a practice of beginning each Monday morning in prayer and fasting, laying the week before God. On Tuesday evenings, they set aside time to pray with stakeholders involved in various interventions. At any point when they encountered a "roadblock," prayer was their first resort. "When we do not know what to do, we pray."

In prayer, God has revealed new direction and calling. He once invited Florence to grasp a fistful of sand and told her that Life in Abundance would train as many leaders as the grains of sand she held in her hand: But Life in Abundance didn't train leaders at the time. They've since trained more than 20,000.

In another instance, God told Florence that Life in Abundance would one day have an aviation company. That hadn't been in her plan, but she invited the team to take that vision to prayer, and years later, it came to pass.[8]

"Visionary prayer," she writes, "influences communities, informs strategies, and sets our God-sized goals—going for more than we can imagine or plan for and continually calling it into being in prayer. We become desperate for God to manifest."

Gil Odendaal has spent his career in leadership roles with global organizations, including global director of HIV/AIDS initiatives at Saddleback Church and senior leadership roles with World Relief and Medical Ambassadors International. He has been involved with Life in Abundance since 2002 and has witnessed firsthand the incredible culture of prayer within the organization. "What Life in Abundance is doing, when you ask how it happened there, I truly believe it is from the top down," he says. "When Florence started this organization, it was literally moving forward on her knees."[9]

"What I've seen with Life in Abundance is that prayer has become part of the culture because there is a deep belief that prayer changes things," Gil says. Their culture of prayer has become a self-sustaining cycle. The more they believe that prayer changes things, the more they pray—and the more they pray, the more things change.

Even when leaders believe in the importance of prayer, it can be difficult to establish a *culture of prayer*. For leaders, this might seem an overwhelming, impossible task, but from our interviews with praying leaders, we have discovered that it is possible to create a culture of prayer, as we'll further explore in the chapters to come.

PRAYER

Be my vision, oh Lord of my Heart.
Be my meditation by day or night.
May it be you that I behold even in my sleep.
Be my speech, be my understanding.
Be with me, may I be with you.
Be my father, may I be your child.
May you be mine, may I be yours.
Be my battle-shield, be my sword.
Be my dignity, be my delight.
Be my shelter, be my stronghold.
Raise me up to the company of the angels.
Be every good to my body and soul.
Be my Kingdom in heaven and on earth.
Be solely the chief love of my heart.
Let there be none other, O high king of heaven,
Until I am able to pass into your hands,
My treasure, my beloved, through the greatness of your love.
Be the constant guardian of every possession and every life,
For our corrupt desires are dead at the mere sight of you.
O king of heaven grant me this:
Your love be in my heart and in my soul.
With the king of all, with him after victory won by piety,
May I be in the kingdom of heaven, O brightness of the sun.
O heart of my heart, whatever befall me,
O ruler of all, be my vision.

—Dallán Forgaill (sixth century)

PRAYER TOOL

STEPS TOWARD A CULTURE OF PRAYER

The following list lays out eight concrete steps for developing a culture of prayer in your organization.

1. Become a praying leader.

Where we find a culture of prayer, it begins with a leader who is dedicated to prayer. E. M. Bounds wrote, "None but praying leaders can have praying followers."[10] The Barna study mentioned in Chapter 1 agrees: Of the ministries that affirm "prayer is a priority," 89 percent say that their leaders "effectively model prayer practices." See more in Chapters 1–4.

2. Pray for those you lead.

Part of a leader's unique responsibility is to uphold team members in prayer, offering gratitude as well as petitions for the team. Your prayers for those you lead can prepare their hearts to embrace a culture of prayer. See Chapter 12.

3. Build teams to pray with and for you.

Leaders of prayer surround themselves with other people of prayer. When John Mark Comer invited me (Cameron) to serve as the founding executive director of Practicing the Way, the first thing we did was gather a prayer team from our church partners and givers. We had a powerful prayer team before we even had a registered 501(c)(3).

Jesus is especially present when groups gather (Matthew 18:19–20). One intercessor who works with the Maclellan Foundation, a Tennessee-based foundation dedicated to serving Christ and His Kingdom, suggests leaders ask the Lord to send intercessors. "Come together to prayer-walk the land—the property, the place. Gather your intercessors for a 'meet and greet' and to cast vision; write it down." See Chapter 13.

4. Model prayer for and with other believers in the organization.

To spread a culture of prayer, the leader doesn't proclaim a program; the leader prays visibly. Next, the leader gathers a small group to pray. Prayer isn't delegable; everything else is (Acts 6:2–4). See Chapters 5–10.

5. Support staff prayer.

Leaders give their teams permission to pray. I have instructed my team that they are welcome to take up to 10 percent of their "on the clock" time to focus solely on prayer. I've also given my team members permission to pause meetings to pray by modeling that practice. See Chapter 14 on investing in prayer.

6. Gather consistently in prayer.

Team members should be free to pray alone, but to build a culture of prayer, the leader should also create space on the calendar for corporate prayer. Through the Word and the leader's modeling, the Holy Spirit will grow the team's passion for prayer. Prayer becomes a key group activity (Acts 20:36) that brings unity (2 Chronicles 5:13–14; Acts 1:13–14), powerful results (Acts 12:5–11), and direction from God (Acts 13:1–3). The ministries most likely to see God moving powerfully through their organizations are those that proactively schedule prayer as a group.

See Chapter 2 on the importance of making a plan to pray consistently. This applies not only at the personal level but also at the organizational level.

7. Devote people and places to prayer.

Since prayer is a "first of all" priority (1 Timothy 2:1–4), ministries demonstrate its primacy by giving it focus. Many begin by appointing a prayer coordinator who intercedes, hosts structured prayer times, and tracks prayer points. Others create spaces dedicated to prayer where staff are welcome to pause their workday and pray. See Chapter 14.

8. Make prayer a line item in your budget.

A quantifiable amount of time and resources must be invested in prayer. Consider adding a line item to your budget to capture these costs and formalize your commitment. Investing time, systems, and money in prayer elevates the organization's commitment and provides greater visibility to prayer. See Chapter 14.

To make prayer easy for your organization, we have partnered with the Echo Prayer app to create "Echo for Ministries." It's a beautiful way to gather, filter, and share prayer requests across your organization. Our organizations have each invested to make this app available to increase the amount and specificity of prayer. Join us at www.leadwithprayer.com!

CHAPTER 12

LEADERS PRAY FOR THOSE THEY LEAD

We constantly pray for you.
—*2 Thessalonians 1:11*

Regi Campbell, the founder of Radical Mentoring, kept a secret that wasn't uncovered until after his death in January 2020.

The world knew Regi as an investor, entrepreneur, and mentor to younger men. He was CEO of four companies and the author of four books. In 2007 he founded Radical Mentoring to grow his mentoring work, and at the time of his death, hundreds of churches had entrusted Radical Mentoring to disciple the men in their congregations.

David Wills, president emeritus of National Christian Foundation, became a dear friend of Regi's. After Regi passed away, one of the young men Regi mentored sent David a photo of something he discovered in their mutual friend's home. The photo was taken in Regi's prayer closet, and it showed a large whiteboard with six columns of names, printed in small, neat letters. The board included the names of every man in every mentoring group that Regi had ever led, dating back to the beginning of Radical Mentoring. Regi's journals and papers made it clear that these names weren't an attendance roster or scoreboard; these names were Regi's prayer list.

"We were amazed," said Wills. "All these men, all these names. You had the sense, standing in Regi's prayer closet, that you were standing on holy ground."[1]

David Sykora oversaw a team working in pharmaceuticals in New Hampshire when he met Regi. He was so motivated to be mentored by Regi that he flew to Atlanta each month to sit at Regi's feet. During those meetings with younger men, Regi would ask someone to pray at the beginning, at the end, and in the middle as specific issues arose.

"When Regi prayed for you," said Sykora, "it was something different. He'd come up to you, and put a hand on you and say, 'Speak, Lord, Your servant is listening.' And the way he talked to God was like a conversation, like he was expecting that God would answer his questions."[2]

Regi shared with these men that he began each day with quiet time with God, including significant time in prayer.

Sykora found that Regi's prayers for him spilled out of the prayer closet and into their conversations. "Regi had a way of knowing the words that would speak most to my heart," said Sykora.

He'd tell you, "Hey, I love you," and it wasn't just "Love you, man," but you felt it and he would stand there and look at you and reiterate it. And the depth of meaning behind that let me know that this wasn't superficial; this was a supernatural love that he had for me and for others he led. And that supernatural love *can't* be formed without prayer. He'd always challenge you in ways that were personal and specific and appropriate to your season. You *have* to be praying for someone to love them like that. And he really wanted to listen to you.

Regi hadn't always been that good at listening to God or others, though.

Early in Regi's career, he was rising quickly in the telecommunications industry. As a high-flying MBA on his way to being named Georgia's "Entrepreneur of the Year," life was moving at breakneck speed. Businesses grew, opportunities arose. One new role required a move to another city, and like many businessmen, Regi accepted the role. But unlike many businessmen, Regi hadn't told his wife about it before agreeing to the move.

By this time, Miriam had seen enough and left Regi. But her leaving removed the scales from Regi's eyes, and shortly after, on his knees in the backyard, he cried out to God and received salvation. As he grew in his faith, he later convinced Miriam that God was changing him. He started to put business in its proper place.

Regi saw miraculous answers to prayer. Once, as his son Ross was driving home from medical school, his tires blew out and the car flipped. Regi got the call on a Sunday morning that Ross had been proclaimed dead. Regi alerted his pastor, who stopped the service, and the moment that Regi's church united in prayer, Ross came to life again. Regi was already becoming a man of prayer, and this miracle poured fuel on the fire.

With his priorities straight, Regi's businesses grew; so did his new faith and his family. As others saw Regi's success, they'd ask him to get coffee as a way to get advice. Regi was great at loving people and asking questions, and so more people asked him for coffee. Realizing that he couldn't invest deeply in all those who desired his time, Regi sought God's direction on what to do.

He prayed and decided, "If people want my time, I can give it to them, but they need to be serious." Regi designed a mentoring program for eight men, and each one would have to apply and be accepted. The group would meet monthly for ten months, and before each meeting the mentees would have to read and prepare. At the end of the program, they'd then go on a retreat together. This became Radical Mentoring, and now thousands of men have experienced the impact.

So when Sykora first asked Regi for coffee, Regi lovingly declined and forced him to apply for the program like everyone else. He did—and that's how David Sykora's name ended up on the bottom of Regi's whiteboard in his prayer closet.

"Regi's prayer life was a lot about how he listened to the Spirit," says Sykora. "Over the course of his life, he went from not listening to Miriam to being an amazing listener: to God, and to Miriam, and to us."

"He would call or text just to say that he was thinking of us," says Sykora. "At our final retreat, he would go around and pray for each person individually. We had two hours for eight guys, so he's praying fifteen minutes over each person. He'd say, 'I'm here, God, to pray for my friend and brother David. What do You have to say to us right now?' And then he'd pause, and say to me 'David, mainly that He wants you to know that He loves you.'"

Before passing in 2020, Regi was sick for four years. Toward the end of that season, someone asked Regi a question about Jesus, and after years of talking to Jesus from his prayer closet, Regi paused and said, "I can't wait to meet him."[3]

Avoiding Entitlement in Prayer

In 1 Timothy 2:1–2, Paul is writing to Timothy and urges that "petitions, prayers, intercession and thanksgiving be made...for kings and all those in authority." The calling to pray for leaders is abundantly clear, and we hope that there are many praying specifically for *you* in your leadership role.

Leaders who know about this calling or this verse, including ourselves, can sometimes slip into an attitude of entitlement, believing that others are called to pray on our behalf and excusing ourselves from reciprocating because of the many pressing demands on our time. Many talks, articles, and sermons have established the need to pray for those in authority, but few have emphasized the need for leaders to pray for those we lead. Many leaders have tried to claim a "free pass" on intentionally praying for their teams.

Scripture shows us a different model. Leaders from the Old Testament to the New continually prayed for those they led. They set the example in praying with fervency and specificity. Consider the following examples.

Moses interceded for the rebellious Israelites in the wilderness (Exodus 32:11–14, 31–32; Numbers 14:13–19), at one point identifying with those he led so deeply that he asked God to inflict the punishment they deserved on him instead.

When Nehemiah heard that Jerusalem's walls were broken down and its gates had been burned, he cried out to God: "Let your ear be attentive and your eyes open to hear the prayer your servant is praying before you *day and night* for your servants, the people of Israel" (Nehemiah 1:6, emphasis added).

In the book of Colossians, the apostle Paul gives one of the greatest endorsements of any biblical leader to an otherwise unknown leader named Epaphras. Epaphras is credited with founding the church in Colossae (Colossians 1:7–8). Paul describes him as "a servant of Christ Jesus" who "is always wrestling in prayer for you" (Colossians 4:12). He's described as someone who agonizes in prayer for the disciples he was leading in Colossae, praying that they would be found worthy and spiritually mature.

Paul's letters—each of which was written to people he led—prominently feature prayers for the early church and specific members of these churches. Though Paul famously instructed prayers for those in leadership, he modeled praying for those he led.

By our own count, we found that Paul mentioned praying, or just prayed in the text of his letters, thirty-six times; sometimes in the present tense and sometimes in past tense. For example, in Ephesians 1:16 Paul writes, "I have not stopped giving thanks for you," and in Colossians 1:9 he says, "We continually ask God to fill you with the knowledge of his will." Of those thirty-six prayers, twenty-nine are focused on the people he's writing to, four are prayers about something else (e.g., 1 Timothy 1:12, "I thank Christ Jesus our Lord, who has given me strength, that he considered me trustworthy, appointing me to his service"), and three are prayers of rejoicing.

Paul isn't handing off his prayer list and delegating the task of praying to his followers. Rather, 80 percent of his prayers are *for* those he leads, and of those twenty-nine prayers for his followers, twelve are prayers of *thanks* for them and seventeen include specific requests that he is lifting to heaven on their behalf. Paul is almost equally focused on thanking God for those he leads as he is on asking God to do things for them.

We often ask God to solve problems for those we lead—and sometimes we feel like those we lead *are* challenges or problems we're asking God to solve—but Paul's example of thanking God for those he leads invites us to do the same. As leaders, let's start by being joyfully grateful for those we lead.

Fighting in Prayer

Christine Caine, founder of A21, a nonprofit working to eradicate human trafficking, has spoken about her misconceptions of intercessory prayer as a young believer. She used to feel that intercession was for extra-holy Christians whose spiritual intensity far surpassed her own, but she has grown to love praying for those she leads.[4]

With hundreds of staff members serving in nineteen offices across fifteen countries, crisis is never far away. Whether due to an unstable government, an outbreak of war, a natural disaster, or a medical crisis, Christine says that without the gift of intercessory prayer she would feel very out of control—because so many of these situations truly are outside her control as a leader. "Intercessory prayer helps me put it back onto the shoulders of the only one who could bear the burden for this."

Christine's model of intercessory prayer employs concentric circles. She begins by praying for those closest to her. "I'm always bringing the needs of my husband, my daughters before the Lord." She likens intercessory prayer to "going to war" for another person, and she regularly goes to war in prayer on behalf of her teammates as well as her family and friends. "And then I'll spread out to my ministry life...We make a list internally within our organization of big things we're praying for as an organization. Very specific things for specific offices in different parts of the world, and then even specific individual needs, family needs, health needs of staff within those offices."

As she prays, Christine mentally travels to Bulgaria, South Africa, Mexico, Ukraine, and other parts of the world where A21 is active, inviting God to work on the needs each team has expressed.

Go for It

Inspired by Christine and the praying leaders in Scripture, I (Ryan) have been on a journey to actively pray for those I lead. Sometimes I tell them;

other times I don't. I start out by just asking God what specifically I should pray for them, and then I listen to God. There are times when God has impressed upon me a specific word, image, or phrase that resonated deeply, even miraculously, with the colleague I was praying for. It's a beautiful adventure to ask God how to pray for those I know and lead.

Recently I was praying for a leader I've mentored for years and felt a distinct sense that I was supposed to text him three words: "Go for it." In an act of courage, I texted him and told him that I had this crazy sense that God wanted him to "Go for it." He got my text and started crying. He had been seeking God for a major directional decision that could affect the course of his life and family. That very morning, he had asked God for a sign. Within the hour, he got my random text that said, "Go for it." He cried tears of joy at the personal love of God that came through a random text.

In my own life, praying for those I lead has proven to be one of the best ways to learn to hear the voice of God. Because there's less personal emotion or inner turmoil to contend with, it's easier to quiet my heart to hear from God on behalf of others.

Unfortunately, we all know specific instances when praying for those we lead has been misused. Indeed some leaders claim "God told me in prayer..." as a way to manage an employee or manipulate others. To prevent any temptation toward this in my own leadership, my rule is to share with my employees what God has shown me only when it is encouraging, strengthening, or confirming of guidance God is giving the person in their walk of faith. No directives of leadership and no portfolio or position changes are conveyed with the language of "God told me to..."

Praying an Org Chart

One way we've begun to implement praying for those we lead has been to print our organizational chart and pray for each individual specifically. Some we know well, and others we interact with less directly, but we've committed to praying for every staff member within our organization.

Praying for personal requests requires a baseline of care and trust. The more we are in relationship with those we lead, the better we can support them with specific, intentional prayers. And if we don't have any idea what to pray for, it may be an invitation to spend more time with them, listening to the joys and challenges they are experiencing.

As our understanding of the role of prayer in leaders' lives has grown, we've become convinced that our prayers for those we lead are more than just a kind or generous gesture to convey our love and care. Our prayers for those we lead are another way we can follow the example of Jesus.

Jesus Prays for His Disciples

In the days leading up to Jesus' crucifixion, it seemed His disciples still didn't "get" His leadership model or mission. In countless ways, Jesus had shown that His Kingdom was unlike any earthly kingdom, but still James and John wanted to secure for themselves places of honor. They wanted to sit in venerable posts at Jesus' right and left hands. Power and position have always been alluring pursuits. The other disciples were angered at the gall of James and John, but Jesus replied, "You know that the rulers of the Gentiles lord it over them, and their high officials exercise authority over them. Not so with you. Instead, whoever wants to become great among you must be your servant, and whoever wants to be first must be your slave—just as the Son of Man did not come to be served, but to serve" (Matthew 20:25–28).

Jesus famously served His disciples by washing their feet, but that's not where He stopped. He went on to pray for His friends. In fact, Jesus' longest recorded prayer in Scripture, in John 17, focuses on His disciples and their protection, sanctification, and unity.

Earlier in John, we get a glimpse into what was behind the foot washing and prayers. It's what was behind every part of His mission: love. John 13:1 says, "Jesus knew that the hour had come for him to leave this world and go to the Father. Having loved his own who were in the world, he loved them to the end." Love for His friends was the source of His prayers.

While we only have a limited number of prayers from Jesus in Scripture, based on what we know and the glimpses they provide into His prayer life, we can assume that He regularly prayed not just for His disciples collectively but also for them individually. We do have one example, in Luke 22:31–32 (NKJV), where Jesus prays specifically for Peter: "Satan has asked for you, that he may sift you as wheat. But I have prayed for you, that your faith should not fail."

An Offer, Not an Imposition

André Mann grew up with a mom who modeled prayer. "She would pray over everyone and everything," he remembers.[5] And her devotion to prayer had a powerful impact not only on him and his family but also on her community in Mexico, where she is referred to as "Santa Wilma" or St. Wilma.

The first miraculous answer to prayer André received was when he was thirty-two years old, living in Uzbekistan. One day his family went to visit an elderly woman who was near death, and in what little Tajik he knew, André prayed over the woman, asking the Lord to heal her. Upon returning to his home later that evening, he felt uncertain that God would actually answer his prayer. "Maybe I shouldn't have been so bold," he fretted.

The next day, André was walking around his neighborhood when suddenly he ran into the same elderly woman whom he had prayed over the night before. Looking rejuvenated, the woman asserted that it was because he prayed in the name of Jesus that she had been healed. André was shocked, and shortly after, a number of people from the town began approaching him and his family, asking for prayer and wanting to learn more about Jesus. Eventually, he and his family became known as "the people who pray."

André believed that the miraculous healing done in the life of the elderly woman had nothing to do with him or his prayer, but rather everything to do with the power of God. André recognized that God had chosen to heal the woman to draw others in the community closer to Jesus.

A number of years later, André and his family were living in Afghanistan. While there, they visited the child of a militiaman at a local hospital. The young boy had a significant amount of water on his brain, and André and his family prayed over the child before he underwent surgery. A month later, the boy's father approached André, telling him that his son had been healed because of his prayer.

André's immediate response to the militiaman was that it had been the doctor's surgery, rather than prayer, that had healed the child. But although the boy's father was not a believer, he quickly rejected André's statement, saying, "No, you prayed in Jesus' name, and I've never heard anyone pray in Jesus' name." The militiaman expressed interest in learning more about Christ, and so André and his family invited him to their home for further conversation.

That conversation turned into forty-five days of discipleship. After only fifteen days of reading and discussion, the man committed his life to Jesus, but he stayed another thirty days to grow in his new faith before returning home. "We have to allow our normal life to be interrupted," André said, "even to the point of huge inconvenience, if we want to see God move the way He can move if we just let Him."

André's prayer life took a different shape when he was in the corporate sector, yet even there, he saw the power of prayer. He has held leadership roles at Procter & Gamble and a variety of global businesses. In this context, he also discovered the power of praying for those he led, modeling the same posture and approach that he had when serving as a missionary. André actively waited for God's direction and would reach out to coworkers when he believed they would be open to prayer. They took notice, and many began asking to join him.

Today, André serves in a variety of leadership roles, praying for his teams in all circumstances. While André never imposes prayer on anyone, he actively offers to pray in corporate settings. "People might not be initially open to hearing the Gospel, but they are likely open to receiving prayer."

André has seen prayer produce a greater sense of collective peace in the hearts of employees. He has seen how the God who healed the elderly woman and the young boy is still answering prayers in miraculous ways today.

PRAYER

For this reason, ever since I heard about your faith in the Lord Jesus and your love for all God's people, I have not stopped giving thanks for you, remembering you in my prayers. I keep asking that the God of our Lord Jesus Christ, the glorious Father, may give you the Spirit of wisdom and revelation, so that you may know him better. I pray that the eyes of your heart may be enlightened in order that you may know the hope to which he has called you, the riches of his glorious inheritance in his holy people, and his incomparably great power for us who believe.

—Ephesians 1:15–19

For this reason I kneel before the Father, from whom every family in heaven and on earth derives its name. I pray that out of his glorious riches he may strengthen you with power through his Spirit in your inner being, so that Christ may dwell in your hearts through faith. And I pray that you, being rooted and established in love, may have power, together with all the Lord's holy people, to grasp how wide and long and high and deep is the love of Christ, and to know this love that surpasses knowledge—that you may be filled to the measure of all the fullness of God. Now to him who is able to do immeasurably more than all we ask or imagine, according to his power that is at work within us, to him be glory in the church and in Christ Jesus throughout all generations, for ever and ever! Amen.

—Ephesians 3:14–21

PRAYER TOOL

PRAY YOUR ORG CHART

If you'd like to start on the journey to more intentional prayer for those you lead, consider printing a staff list or organizational chart. Dedicate and set apart a time on your calendar for earnest prayer for your colleagues.

Here are four ways to pray with specificity for those you lead:

1. Pray for the children of those you lead.

One of the best practices I (Ryan) have instituted is to pray not only for my direct reports but also for their children, by name, every day. I have found this incredibly encouraging for my staff. As one leader shared, "I'm grateful when you do something nice for me, but I will never forget you if you do something nice for my kids." Few acts say "I genuinely care for you" more than praying for the children of your closest team members every day.

2. Pray blessings on those you lead.

The most common prayer that leaders pray for those they lead is a blessing—blessing their lives, their families, and their relationship with God.

The second most common prayer is to pray for the spiritual development of those they lead. Pray for spiritual growth and a relationship with Jesus.

3. Empathize in prayer for those you lead.

When Paul talked about one of his praying leaders, Epaphras, he said he "is always *struggling* in prayer on your behalf" (Colossians 4:12 NET). The word *struggle* is where we get the word *agonize*. Praying takes commitment, time, and intentionality, but it also takes empathy and heart, letting ourselves feel the pain of those we lead.

4. Pray Scripture over those you lead.

One of the most powerful ways to pray for those you lead is to pray Scripture over them. If you'd like to start this adventure, begin with prayers in Ephesians 1 and 3, Philippians 1, and Colossians 1.

CHAPTER 13

LEADERS BUILD TEAMS TO PRAY WITH AND FOR THEM

Pray also for me.
—*Ephesians 6:19*

The guards knew me!" Shalom laughed as he told us about the early days of his faith.

After converting to Christianity as a teenager, Shalom began spending three or four nights a week praying overnight at his church. He'd bring a Bible, a small carpet for kneeling, and sometimes one or two friends. "We would pray that God would use us," he says, and as they did, the guards of the church where he prayed became familiar with these young praying teenagers.

When God called Shalom to be His witness "to the ends of the earth" (Acts 1:8), Shalom didn't even know where to find the capital city of Ethiopia, his home country. "I hadn't traveled even fifty kilometers from my home," he remembers.

As we mentioned in Chapter 2, Shalom founded a powerful ministry that has reached thousands for Christ, but the foundation for this movement was laid by Shalom's teenage prayer team.

Now, many years later, Shalom's movement includes 2,000 volunteer intercessors, thirty prayer bases, and ten paid prayer coordinators. As the demands of his ministry have increased, Shalom has formally invited others to support the ministry in prayer. His personal prayer team prays together every morning at eight-thirty for forty minutes. They fast every Wednesday. Four times a year, they fast for three days, and twice a year they fast for six days. "We pray until the impossible happens," he says.

And they've seen the impossible happen.

When a senior leader was conducting an evangelistic training in a region of Ethiopia hostile to the Gospel, an angry mob surrounded the house where they'd gathered, shaking the locked doors and yelling for the leader and his trainees to come out. This leader recognized the danger in this situation, knowing that others had been injured or even killed in similar circumstances. His first call wasn't to the police, because the police were already there. *They had joined the mob.* Instead he called the ministry's lead prayer coordinator. She mobilized a team of intercessors, and miraculously, within the hour, a military van burst through the crowd, saving the leader and trainees.

Shalom's team has embraced the "impossible"—and sometimes unpopular—goal of reaching an especially difficult to reach group of 7.5 million individuals. The Joshua Project, a leading missionary research organization, estimates that just 0.05 percent of this ethnic group were evangelical Christians, but now, in part because of the work Shalom and his team have bathed in prayer, the Gospel is spreading rapidly.

For Shalom's team, expansion into a new region or people group is always preceded by prayer. As the launch draws near, they mobilize prayer teams to pray through the night. "Among this unreached people group, we prayed for ten years," Shalom says. And when Shalom's team shared the Gospel, so many wanted to become disciples that they had to construct a mobile baptismal pool. Now there's a movement of more than one hundred churches among this "unreached" people group.

A lot can happen in a decade of prayer. Health crises come and go. Loved ones enter the world, while others leave it. Some days our prayers will focus not on our grander mission but simply on getting through the valley. This is why a prayer team matters.

Scripture paints a picture of prayer in Exodus. The famous story starts with an intense battle between the Israelites and the Amalekites, with Moses high on a hill raising his arms heavenward (Exodus 17:8–13). When his strength began to flag and his arms began to droop, the battle would turn in favor of the Amalekites, but as long as Moses' arms were raised, the Israelites were winning. As the battle raged on, Moses could not maintain this posture alone; he needed Aaron and Hur to hold up his hands and steady him.

A prayer team figuratively does what Aaron and Hur literally did for Moses. Their support steadies and undergirds leaders, helping them to persevere in prayer and service, lifting them to heaven.

Many of our global friends mentioned the pivotal role of their prayer teams.

- "I have personal intercessors that I pray with...One friend from church...was always a step ahead in what God was showing her in prayer and getting results in prayer."
- "Most of what I learned about prayer was through praying with my personal intercessors."
- "We have regular intercessors behind us from our home church... They're faithful, and they ask for monthly prayer requests."
- "I went to our team and said, 'We need to pray a bold prayer. We've shared with thousands of people, but let's pray that God gives us millions of people'...and God did."

A Communal Invitation

The global Church seems to have grasped Jesus' emphasis on communal prayer. Jesus modeled group prayer, directed group prayer, and promised to show up at group prayer. We know that "where two or three gather" in prayer, Jesus is there (Matthew 18:20), and "If two of you on earth agree about anything they ask for, it will be done for them by my Father in heaven" (Matthew 18:19).

While Jesus often withdrew to pray, many of these "personal" prayer times still included others, like one instance described in Luke 9:18 "when Jesus was praying in private and his disciples were with him." Jesus was praying in private, with His disciples.

In another instance, when Jesus had been praying individually, "One of his disciples said to him, 'Lord, teach us to pray, just as John taught his disciples'" (Luke 11:1). Jesus responded with the Lord's Prayer. Because Jesus' private prayer happened in proximity to a group, we have the Lord's Prayer.

Author and former pastor John Onwuchekwa observes that all the pronouns in the Sermon on the Mount are singular in form ("You are the salt of the earth," "If you love those who love you," "When you give to the needy") except when Jesus is talking about prayer.[1] Then He uses plural forms. In the southern United States, Jesus' words on prayer would be translated "When y'all pray" and "This then is how y'all should pray" (Matthew 6:5, 9).

Prayer teams are thriving in communal cultures around the world, but in the United States, we often think of prayer as a personal pursuit. A Barna Group research study conducted in 2017 reflected that 94 percent of American adults who had prayed in the previous three months most often did so alone.[2] Coincidentally, 94 percent of Google image search results for "prayer" are images of a single person praying.[3]

When we in the West think of prayer, most of us probably picture ourselves alone, but this trend toward independent prayer is a departure from what Jesus modeled, what the early church practiced, and how global leaders continue to pray.

Is it time leaders took their prayer closet experience to the prayer conference room?

The Prayer Team of a Ministry Leader

"If I submit my prayer requests late, I get calls from eighty-year-old women asking for them!" says Peter Kubasek, a Cincinnati, Ohio–based investment banker.[4]

Every weekend for fifteen years, Peter has shared with a team of forty dedicated intercessors a list of challenges he's facing, and among this group are some very consistent and insistent octogenarians. "I don't think I've missed two weeks in fifteen years," he says. He's also made his calendar accessible to the team so they can pray over each week's meetings.

Peter is a powerful ministry leader—and investment banking is his ministry. He has been closely involved in more than 500 merger and acquisition projects, deals valued in the billions of dollars. His thriving company fuels radical generosity, advancing Kingdom causes around the world.

An eighty-three-year-old intercessor first taught Peter the importance of praying the blood of Jesus. "When you're entering a battle," she said, "you need to have the blood of Jesus prayed over you." So daily, before he begins his high-pressure days, Peter prays the blood of Jesus and the armor of God over himself and his family. In addition to his own prayers, Peter invites his team of intercessors to pray for him, his family, and his business.

Peter started his company in 1990 with the commitment to furthering the Kingdom through his profits. Trusted friends told him, "You'd better bathe this in prayer because the business you're trying to start will put a stick in the eye of the devil."

If Peter was going to live at odds with the devil, he knew he needed a team of faithful prayer partners, but Peter wasn't sure how to bathe his business in prayer. He called several Christian business leaders he knew for advice. With pen poised and paper in hand, he asked, "What's your prayer strategy?" But there wasn't much to write down. "Most don't have a prayer strategy, and that's challenging!" says Peter.

Peter looked for a consultant who could help him create a prayer strategy for an organization he was helping to start. That then culminated in twelve business and ministry leaders spending a day in prayerful consideration of how Peter and the new organization could strategically integrate prayer. Together, they determined to hire a prayer coordinator and seven intercessors. "We have layers of prayer and the unbelievable experience of gathering prayer from others," Peter says, describing his volunteer intercessors, paid intercessors, praying teammates, and personal prayers.

Peter prays with participants—even nonbelievers!—before many meetings. During meetings, he's known to pause and take a moment to ask God, "What are we supposed to do here?" Peter's business team prays together often. As a team, "We capture what we're thankful for, and we listen."

Peter's commitment to prayer doesn't mean that his business always runs smoothly. In 2012, Peter was diagnosed with skin cancer. While Peter was recuperating from surgery, it was discovered that an associate had been stealing the rent check for months, and Peter's firm was evicted from its offices. The US Securities and Exchange Commission subpoenaed Peter about one of his business partners' activities, and that person was indicted. "There were probably six or eight other things that were each extraordinary," he remembers of the challenging season. "Everything was going wrong."

As Peter transparently and vulnerably leaned into his prayer team, God began to move in the unseen. "We would have been bankrupt if we didn't close five deals; we closed five deals in the fourth quarter and made more than we ever had. It was God's sufficiency." Others in Peter's sphere—especially nonbelievers—were amazed to see God deliver the firm from ruin.

While Peter doesn't pray for money for its own sake, he does pray for the chance to be generous.

Peter is both living and modeling a prayerful life as he incorporates prayer teams in a secular context, but his model of an intercessory team supporting his leadership is not the only approach to prayer teams.

A Staff Team That's Also a Prayer Team

In Asunción, Paraguay, Judah Mooney runs Diaconía, a nonprofit that provides Christ-centered financial services and educational workshops to Paraguayan women with limited access to capital and basic business training. With nearly a quarter of Paraguay's population living in poverty, the need can feel overwhelming.

"When you live outside of the realm of what you can do by yourself, you understand that in order to do this thing that God has asked you to do, you need God," Judah says. Humble recognition of his own insufficiency helped Judah grow as a person of prayer. "As I encountered people in situations of sickness and poverty, I as Judah Mooney was not able to resolve these problems—but God had the answer, and God always has the answer for humanity's need." In prayer, Judah confessed, "God, I can't do this. What would You do?"

Judah says he's grown to anticipate that God will graciously involve him in His plan for the answer. "I'm continually asking, how can I position myself to be part of Your restorative plan? What are You doing here, and how do I align myself to Your plan in this situation?"

Part of that alignment meant involving his team in prayer. Many Diaconía staff members were already dedicated to prayer personally. One employee set an alarm to sound every fifteen minutes to remind himself to pause and become aware of the Holy Spirit's work in that moment, continuing until the habit was so ingrained that he no longer needed the alarm's reminder to prompt his thoughts heavenward. But in 2018, Diaconía's leadership team formalized prayer as a core value for the organization. "We pray because it is God who transforms lives," they affirm.

"God is at work, and God is good. We pray because we believe He's restoring people and answering prayers all the time," Judah says.

Diaconía's entire staff spend time praying collectively over both work and personal needs. Each morning begins with a fifteen-minute meeting that includes a prayer need of the day. Once a week the team comes together for an extended prayer time, lifting up colleagues and clients, budgets, training plans, and strategic decisions. They bring everything before the Father because they wholeheartedly believe that He is the answer to the challenges facing Diaconía, their clients, and their staff members. Monthly, they gather together for praise and worship, honoring God and celebrating His faithfulness by sharing testimonies of where they have seen Him at work. They also practice regular rhythms of review, looking back to past prayer requests to celebrate God's provision and to persevere in prayer over challenges that remain.

"We don't just start meetings in prayer as a formality," Judah says. "As a team we understand that it is God who transforms lives."[5]

Three Approaches to Team Prayer

In our conversations with praying leaders, we discovered three distinct kinds of prayer groups, often with overlapping functions: *personal teams, organization-focused teams,* and *outward-facing teams.*

Personal teams are often smaller and convene to pray specifically for a leader and his/her family and work. Peter Kubasek's intercessors are one example of a personal team.

Organization-focused teams are generally larger, inclusive of the organization's staff, and focused on praying for the organization's team, fruitfulness, and finances. Staff members at Diaconía comprise an organization-focused prayer team.

Outward-facing teams are convened by a ministry for the purpose of praying for the ministry's constituents, like Shalom's team praying for a decade before reaching out to a specific unreached people group in Ethiopia.

Prayer in the Early Church

Group prayer pops up on most pages of Acts. The disciples devoted themselves to prayer (Acts 2). When the distribution of food to widows required more staff, the disciples stopped to pray and discern (Acts 6). When Peter was in prison, people *gathered* to pray (Acts 12). The list goes on and on.[6]

In *more than half* of Paul's thirteen letters, he asks for prayer in these same categories: himself, his ministry, and those to whom he ministers. Paul doesn't wait for everyone to become spiritually mature in order to invite their prayers. He wants *everyone* to pray, so he is not shy in asking others to intercede!

Here's what his prayer points look like:

- *For boldness.* "Pray also for me, that whenever I speak, words may be given me so that I will fearlessly make known the mystery of the gospel" (Ephesians 6:19).
- *That the Gospel spreads.* "As for other matters, brothers and sisters, pray for us that the message of the Lord may spread rapidly and be honored" (2 Thessalonians 3:1).
- *For safety and favor.* "Join me in my struggle by praying to God for me. Pray that I may be kept safe from the unbelievers in Judea and that the contribution I take to Jerusalem may be favorably received by the Lord's people there" (Romans 15:30–31).

- *That the message is proclaimed clearly.* "And pray for us, too, that God may open a door for our message, so that we may proclaim the mystery of Christ, for which I am in chains. Pray that I may proclaim it clearly, as I should" (Colossians 4:3–4).
- *That they uphold one another in prayer.* "Always keep on praying for all the Lord's people" (Ephesians 6:18).
- *General request for prayer.* "Brothers and sisters, pray for us" (1 Thessalonians 5:25).

The Gift of a Prayer Team

In 2016, a group called African Strategic Leaders Prayer Network kindly offered to meet with me (Cameron) for prayer. They proposed to meet every week for an hour. As a busy, task-oriented, Type A, Enneagram 3, praying that much was new to me. When we began, I confess that I would listen on the phone while working through emails, offering the occasional "Yes" or "Amen."

Over time, I came to see the beauty of the gift that this team was offering me. After a few months of weekly prayer, they declared, "Okay, now that we've established a prayer canopy over you, we can move to just praying together once a month." Continuing to this day, I call in to a conference line the first Thursday of each month and walk through my neighborhood as my dear friends Keziah, Abi, Emanuel, and Grace pray. They hear my prayer update for about five minutes, taking careful notes. Then Abi leads the team in a couple of worship songs, and each team member prays through my prayer points for about ten minutes each. Mid-month, I send them an updated list of itemized prayer points.

My personal prayer team has been absolutely revolutionary to my prayer life, and God continuously and miraculously opens doors in response to these great people of prayer. Their phrases have become my own; their prayer life is becoming mine, and the gift of this prayer team continues to bless me and others.

PRAYER

Take my life and let it be
consecrated, Lord, to thee.
Take my moments and my days;
let them flow in endless praise,
let them flow in endless praise.
Take my hands and let them move
at the impulse of thy love.
Take my feet and let them be
swift and beautiful for thee,
swift and beautiful for thee.
Take my voice and let me sing
always, only, for my King.
Take my lips and let them be
filled with messages from thee,
filled with messages from thee.
Take my silver and my gold;
not a mite would I withhold.
Take my intellect and use
every power as thou shalt choose,
every power as thou shalt choose.
Take my will and make it thine;
it shall be no longer mine.
Take my heart it is thine own;
it shall be thy royal throne,
it shall be thy royal throne.
Take my love; my Lord, I pour
at thy feet its treasure store.
Take myself, and I will be
ever, only, all for thee,
ever, only all for thee.

—*Frances R. Havergal*

PRAYER TOOL

STEPS TO BUILDING PERSONAL PRAYER TEAMS

There are two main types of prayer teams.

1. Small prayer team: a small, select group that prays for one another.
    Example:

    Jesus invited a small, close group—Peter, James, and John—to join
    Him in prayer before facing the cross (Matthew 26:37–38).
2. Large prayer team: a broad group of intercessors who feel called to lift
    you up in prayer.
    Example:

    The apostle Paul frequently invited—even pleaded for!—the
    churches receiving his letters to pray for him (see Romans 15:30–32;
    Ephesians 6:18–20; Colossians 4:2–4; 1 Thessalonians 5:25; 2 Thes-
    salonians 3:1–2).

Steps to Create a Small Prayer Team

1. Pick your team.

Choose a group of three to five people for whom you can pray, who
will also commit to praying for you. This group must comprise people you
can trust with personal prayer requests.

They should be:

- People of humility and character who love to pray.
- People you would love to pray with and for.
- People without ulterior motives or agendas.
- People who can maintain confidentiality and be trusted implicitly.

2. Set a rhythm.

- Ask these three to five individuals to commit to praying for you and
  with you.
- Commit to one year initially; renew your commitment one year at a
  time.
- Set a regular time to connect either online or in person for prayer.

3. Establish open communication.
   - Communicate what you would like them to pray for.
   - Give them prayer resources like books, prayer cards, Scriptures, and ancient prayers to pray for you, etc.
   - Share real-time requests but also share regularly on a monthly or weekly basis.
   - Celebrate wins, share praises, and offer updates on previous prayer requests so they can see how God is working through their prayers for you.
4. Thank them regularly.
   - Give them a small gift, send a handwritten note, or treat them to a meal.
   - Make sure they feel appreciated and know that their prayers are making a difference.

Steps to Create a Large Prayer Team

This is a larger group of people with whom you can communicate through group email, a closed group on social media, text messaging, or some other form of group communication.

This group by and large does not need to be screened. You can issue a broad invitation for people who feel called to pray for you to join this group. Because this is a larger group, your prayer requests will naturally be more ministry- and leadership-focused and less personal.

1. Send out the call.
   - Send out a broad request for people to join your prayer team.
   - Lay out the expectations (join for one year, receive monthly or weekly requests, etc.).
2. Establish open communication.
   - Communicate what you would like them to pray for.
   - Give them prayer resources like books, prayer cards, Scriptures, and ancient prayers to pray for you, etc.
   - Share real-time requests but also share regularly on a monthly or weekly basis.

- Celebrate wins, share praises, and offer updates on previous prayer requests so they can see how God is working through their prayers for you.

3. Thank them regularly.
   - Give them small gifts or send a handwritten note to members of your prayer team on a rotating basis.
   - Make sure they feel appreciated and know that their prayers are making a difference.

CHAPTER 14

LEADERS INVEST IN PRAYER

The key to the rest of our life and ministry will be the investment of prayer.

—*W. A. Criswald*

We invest hundreds of thousands of dollars in prayer every year. If it is important, it must be a line item in the budget!" Jon Tyson asserted in a thick Australian accent. Jon is a pastor at Church of the City New York in downtown Manhattan, just off Times Square: one of the busiest intersections in one of the busiest cities in the world. Surrounded by the raging lights of Times Square with millions of people rushing here and there, Jon intentionally creates a monastic-like praying community in his church, where he, his staff, and congregants choose to be still before God and seek His will in prayer. Jon's vision is to create an epicenter of prayer in the heart of New York City.

But to achieve this, Jon realizes that he has to invest financially. Each year he allocates a significant portion of his church's budget—hundreds of thousands of dollars—to prayer. He allocates resources to create physical spaces that are conducive to prayer, hires dedicated prayer coordinators, pays his staff to be at prayer meetings throughout the week, and sponsors other pastors to come learn about prayer at his church.

Jon says that he takes seriously the words of Jesus: "My house will be called a house of prayer for all nations" (Mark 11:17), and Jon shows this seriousness with his investments.

I (Ryan) have been inspired by Jon's example, and after speaking with him I realized that VENTURE's budget simply did not show that we valued prayer—and that needed to change. We made the decision that prayer will not just be a priority of our culture at VENTURE but it will be a line item in our budget. We've since invested in 24/7 prayer rooms, prayer coordinators, and prayer gatherings in some of the least-reached countries in the world.

Since we launched a 24/7 prayer room in Southeast Asia, the pace of planting churches there has doubled, the government granted land to one of the lowest-caste groups for the first time in 300 years, and one of our team members was able to share the Gospel face-to-face with the nation's president for more than an hour. These breakthroughs can all be traced to prayers prayed in the 24/7 prayer room. (We've enlisted people in our prayer rooms around the world to pray for everyone who reads this book, too.)

Jon's passion to invest in prayer comes out of a life of passionate prayer. He spends up to three hours per day in Scripture, devotional reading, prayer, and intercession. His morning each day is focused on communion, connection, worship, listening, Scripture, meditation, and delighting in the presence of Jesus. Throughout the day he holds prayer meetings with his team, and at night he devotes time for intercession.

Jon says that he wants to help "bend Western culture toward revival," and his study of history convinced him that there is no way to see this happen apart from first launching a prayer movement. Jon takes inspiration from the Moravian mission movement of the 1700s, one of the longest continuous prayer meetings in history.

The One-Hundred-Year Prayer Meeting

One of the most significant investments in prayer in the history of the church is an effort that came to be known as the one-hundred-year prayer meeting.

Count Nikolaus Ludwig von Zinzendorf, a wealthy aristocrat and passionate Christ follower, was one key leader of this effort, which began in the early 1700s in Saxony, Germany.

At around that time, the Moravians, a group of passionate, missions-minded Protestants, were being persecuted by the Catholic Church, and Nikolaus was moved by their plight. He offered hundreds asylum in his estate, and they called the missional community that formed Herrnhut (The Watch of the Lord).

Nikolaus then left his position in the court of the king and devoted himself to investing in this community, which happened to be a community that prayed. On August 13, 1727, while praying, an "unusual grace" came upon all of them. In many journals we have from the community, this moment was called a "Pentecost."[1] As a result, the community committed to around-the-clock prayer. They would take turns together or alone, covering every hour of the day in prayer, inspired by Leviticus 6:13, which says, "The fire must be kept burning on the altar continuously."

This continued nonstop for more than one hundred years.

Nikolaus invested his considerable fortune in the community and this prayer effort. Today many missiologists view this prayer meeting as the fire that sparked the modern missions revolution that continues to this day, having influenced such leaders as William Carey, who is regarded as "The Father of Modern Missions," and John Wesley, the founder of the Methodist Church. Nikolaus's investment helped changed the face of Christianity around the world.

Prayer Investment in Practice

Shalom puts a large part of his budget toward prayer, sponsoring a day-long prayer gathering of 200,000 people. There is no stage or presentation, just 200,000 people collectively praying for God to change their nation and the nations of the world. It's indeed a significant investment to provide the coordination, volunteers, food for the workers before and afterward, marketing, and all of the expenses one could imagine for an event of this scale. But Shalom says, "It's worth it."

In 2021, a group of Western donors asked Shalom to send them a proposal for church planting among the unreached, and they were a bit perplexed by the proposed budget he sent back. The donors were used to seeing line items for gas, computers, and trainers to travel from place to place. But when they saw Shalom's budget, they noted that *almost half* of it was dedicated to prayer coordinators and prayer gatherings. "Of course," Shalom responded immediately over Zoom. "You said you wanted to focus on unreached groups, and that never happens without a lot of people doing a lot of praying." The group approved the request.

Since then, prayers to God have changed the spiritual dynamics of that area, and the project has shifted toward church planting and training. For mature projects, Shalom dedicates around 10 percent of the budget to prayer. "God always moves in the spiritual realm before He moves in the physical realm," he says.

Investing in Prayer at a For-Profit Company

Jay Martin, founder of Martin Bionics, has innovated prosthetics for amputees that fit like sneakers, providing unprecedented comfort and a transformed quality of life. Their breakthrough technology has impacted the prosthetics industry in the United States and also given Martin Bionics the opportunity to serve those in poverty throughout the developing world.

Jay, who previously designed exoskeleton suits for space and military applications for NASA, has known the importance of depending on God in all aspects of life since childhood. But it wasn't until he faced medical challenges in college that he learned how to press in to the Lord. Jay prayed fervently for miraculous healing. At first, it didn't seem as though his prayers were making a difference, but he continued to trust the Father and remain steadfast in prayer.

With time, Jay began seeing spiritual breakthroughs. In some instances, he heard the Lord speaking to him directly; in others, fellow believers spoke into his life prophetically. These encounters not only revealed God's power in new ways to Jay but also awakened an ever-growing hunger to know God more.

After about two years of pressing in to God through prayer, Jay was completely and miraculously healed. Through that miraculous healing experience, God's presence had become so tangible that he continued to pursue God's will and experience His presence in other facets of life.

Years later, after Jay had founded and grown Martin Bionics, he became even more intrigued with the depth of impact that prayer could play in a business. He connected with Pastor Jon Tyson, who showed him a white paper produced by the Maclellan Foundation that described their prioritization of prayer in organizational settings. In the weeks to come, Jay felt stirred to begin formally implementing prayer within his company.

Jay hired Sandra, a gifted intercessor he knew, to serve as a part-time corporate intercessor within his company. Jay asserts that the company's overall success that year was "directly correlated to having her on staff."[2] Sandra spent dedicated time each day praying over everything from patient schedules and important business decisions to individual staff members. Specific direction that God provided through Sandra helped Jay make counterintuitive company decisions that proved fruitful and ultimately enabled Martin Bionics to impact many more lives.

One day Sandra shared with Jay that she sensed God encouraging him to make decisions based on His leading rather than on what makes the most business sense, and that his "yes" needed to remain a "yes." Earlier that same day Jay had canceled a speaking engagement that he had previously committed to at an upcoming prosthetics conference because it "didn't make good business sense." After he heard from Sandra, he knew the word was about that decision, so he reversed course and decided to speak at the conference after all.

After the conference, Jay was approached by a man who had helped construct a prosthetics clinic that Martin Bionics partnered with in Haiti. After conversing for a short time, the two decided that Martin Bionics would acquire a clinic the man owned in Austin, Texas. This became Martin Bionics's first domestic clinic outside their Oklahoma City base. Jay didn't know at the time of the acquisition that the revenue from the new Austin clinic would have a massive impact on the company's overall prosperity that year. None of it would have been possible without Sandra's prayerful discernment and Jay's willingness to follow God's lead.

After seeing the impact of corporate prayer within the company, Jay expanded the intercessory prayer team. Each part-time prayer team member covered a portion of the workday. Jay later formed a spiritual advisory board, bringing together individuals with gifts of prophecy, discernment, and intercession among others. Together they prayerfully provided input about what they sensed God wanted to do within the company.

Sometime later, Martin Bionics had an opportunity to buy out some early investors after the investors raised concerns about the company's prayer practices. Jay wholeheartedly believed their prayerful culture was honoring God, but he desperately needed funds to keep the company afloat and to buy out these investors. Jay turned to God in prayer. Days later, he got a call from a firm offering a sizable investment. Martin Bionics received the funds right on time: the day before they were needed for the buyout. More importantly, though, these events revealed the power of faithful reliance on the Lord, once again reinforcing the company's conviction of living in deep dependence on God.

Martin Bionics has also experienced a number of miraculous healings. One day, the CFO of Martin Bionics was in town for a business meeting and was suffering from a massive migraine. Though in excruciating pain, the CFO pledged to attend the meeting at a local café. Jay offered to pray over the CFO, who was not a believer, asking that his migraine would disappear as soon as he entered the café. And that is exactly what happened. The CFO marveled that when he walked through the door, his migraine suddenly and completely disappeared. Humorously, when he walked back through the door of the café to exit, it returned. Jay prayed for him again, and the headache was again healed. Several other staff and patients have been healed through prayer as well. Chronic migraines vanished, shoulder injuries disappeared, back pain was eliminated, phantom limb pain was reduced, and one woman who was paralyzed walked again. In Jay's eyes, however, these healing miracles—while certainly awe-inspiring—are only "the first rung on the ladder" of what God is able to do within the company.

Beyond the visible impacts of intercessory prayer, Jay began considering how other spiritual gifts could play into the company's practices, such as using the gift of discernment when hiring new staff.

Not everyone who works at Martin Bionics is a believer or a proponent of spiritual giftings. Nonetheless, Jay longs for more of his colleagues to experience the fullness of what God is able to do.

Jay acknowledges that not all Christians value or practice prayer in the workplace, sometimes because they simply don't realize it's an option. Those who do recognize that spiritual disciplines can be incorporated into business settings are often uncertain about where to start, as was the case with Jay early in his company's journey. Others have not yet come to realize that the full scope of what the Lord is able to do in the workplace goes far beyond weekly Bible studies or posters with Scripture adorning the walls.

Despite these misconceptions and presumed minefields, Jay longs for other believers in the business world to realize the extent of what God can do within a business. By pursuing and partnering with what the Lord is doing, we can truly envision the reality of "on earth as it is in heaven" (Matthew 6:10). Jay finds intrinsic value in inviting God to participate in the workplace, and he unashamedly admits that his company has only survived because of the Lord's provision and compassion for amputees.

In the future, Jay hopes to conduct a clinical study on prayer at Martin Bionics's clinics to quantify the effects of prayer on patients who suffer from phantom limb pain. It is his sincerest desire that one day Martin Bionics will be known not only as a company that provides quality prosthetics but also as a place of healing, where individuals experience the Father's love, compassion, and provision.

Prioritizing Prayer

As we spoke with praying leaders about their commitment to building cultures of prayer, we heard about investments of staff positions, systems, and funding.

Some praying leaders—like Shalom, Jay Martin, Joni Eareckson Tada, and Peter Kubasek—have hired dedicated staff members to organize and coordinate their organizational prayer efforts. Others have invested in systems that reinforce their commitment to prayer.

Praxis is a venture-building ecosystem, bringing together founders, funders, and innovators whose faith motivates them to address the major issues of our time. They exist to equip and resource redemptive entrepreneurship, and the innovators they serve are tackling challenges like racial injustice, climate change, and inequity in educational opportunity.

Mary Elizabeth Ellett, Praxis's chief of staff, has led the organization's prayer practices for more than five years.[3] From the company's founding, staff prayer was prioritized, but as the community grew, they needed a system to ensure that they followed through on commitments made to pray for members of their community.

To ensure this important priority is not overlooked, the Praxis team created an automated process to help Mary Elizabeth solicit requests for prayer from Praxis's community. On a staggered basis, she emails more than 500 people, recording their prayer requests in a database. During each day's staff prayer time, specific people are prayed for. Over the course of a year, every person in the Praxis community has been invited to submit prayer requests and has been intentionally prayed over.

The emails are short, clear, and encouraging:

Greetings from Praxis! We pray for members of our community throughout the year, and about a week from now we will be praying for you personally during our daily team prayer time.

We would love to intercede for you, or give thanks alongside you, in specific ways, so please let me know if there is anything you'd like our team to know as we pray for you during this challenging season.

Don't worry at all if you don't have time to reply—we will pray for you, with thanksgiving, either way!

Praxis's system ensures that their stated value of prayer is actively and consistently practiced.

It seems impossible to significantly invest in prayer as an organization without a financial investment. It may be by investing in additional space for prayer, like a dedicated building or room; by creating opportunities for prayer, like the prayer gatherings that Shalom and Jon Tyson host;

or by freeing staff—and this seems necessary—to dedicate some of their working hours to prayer. This is true even among organizations that have a specific role and individual dedicated to prayer. Joni Eareckson Tada says that every staff member of Joni and Friends is responsible for praying.

Jesus reminds us, "Where your treasure is, there your heart will be also" (Matthew 6:21). It is impossible to treasure Jesus in our hearts without following up with investing our physical treasure. There is a connection between our hearts and our finances. Investing our hearts in relationship with God includes investing our finances in prayer.

A Multimillion-Dollar Investment in Prayer

Gary Haugen, CEO and founder of International Justice Mission (IJM), has said that when we say that something matters, we could mean two different things.

The first meaning is we value this thing. It matters to us, like our marriage or our home. These are things we cherish.

The second meaning is this thing makes a difference. For example, it matters to bring sunscreen to the beach or a flashlight on a camping trip. It matters to an outcome that we value—in these cases, not getting a blistering sunburn or tripping over an unseen branch.

Gary compellingly argues that prayer matters not only in this first way, in which it's valuable to us, but also in the second, in which it actually influences outcomes in real-world struggles.

"We at IJM affirm with everything in our being that prayer matters. It matters of course because God matters. He's the creator, He's the prime mover, He's the Lord over all the earth, over all history, over all time and space. He is indeed the God of justice. The God of all mercy. The God of compassion."[4] This conviction drives a deep commitment to prayer at IJM.

Few organizations have a clearer or grander mission than IJM. For more than twenty-five years, IJM staff around the world have worked with local authorities to rescue and protect tens of thousands of people in poverty from violent forms of oppression such as labor trafficking, sexual exploitation, police abuse of power, and violence against women and children. By 2030, IJM seeks to rescue millions and protect half a billion of the world's most vulnerable from ever experiencing this kind of violent exploitation in the first place. They have drive and ambition, backed up by results.

I (Peter) and the rest of HOPE International's leadership team wanted to learn from IJM how they've implemented organizational prayer, and so we arranged for an exchange visit. Arriving at eight thirty a.m. on the dot, stepping off the elevator, we found an eerily silent office. We almost wondered if we had come on the wrong day or turned up in the wrong spot, but we soon realized that every IJM employee—in every office around the world—begins their day with thirty minutes of silent prayer at their desks. As the day began, they were inviting God into it, starting with stillness, not their emails.

At eleven a.m. the full office paused again so the entire staff could join together in corporate prayer.

The organizational commitment to prayer is not confined to their set-apart prayer times each day. Staff members also partake in office-wide prayer retreats each quarter. A workday (typically a Friday) is spent in a simple, thematic teaching, worship, and two hours of guided reflection. In addition, all members of the IJM team spend one workday a year in personal solitude and reflection. Prayer guides and materials are provided for these personal prayer days, along with accountability from the organization's management, who make sure that every individual schedules their day of reflection and prayer.

About 14 percent of IJM staff's time is spent in spiritual formation, and this devotion to prayer comes with a real cost. It's a significant investment of time that last year translated to an investment of roughly $4 million globally.[5] But Gary and the leadership team view it as an essential expenditure.

Daily liturgies and practices of prayer serve as helpful reminders to Gary and other IJM staff members that the miracles they hope to one day see in the world are ultimately not the result of their own work but of God's grace breaking through.

"As Jesus relentlessly taught us, God in His sovereignty has chosen not to do all of this on His own. Rather God has chosen to give us a part to play in things that really matter. God allows us to impact real events, both by the work we do and through unleashing His power into the world through our asking," Gary reflects. "We cannot choose to matter more than God has ordained. That would be pride. But we can choose to matter less than He has ordained by declining His invitation to release His power into the world through prayer."[6]

At the end of the day, IJM believes that it is God who transforms hearts and takes care of the truly "big" issues in the world—a humbling and freeing reminder.

There is a real financial cost to the way praying leaders supported personal and organizational prayer, but they see it as a worthwhile investment. Mysteriously and miraculously, God turns this "loss" into a gain.

PRAYER

Grant to us, Lord,
that we may set our hope on Your name
which is the primal source of all creation,
and open the eyes of our hearts,
that we may know You,
who alone dwells in the highest heavens,
holy in the holy,
who lays low the insolence of the proud,
who sets the lowly on high,
and brings the lofty low,
the Creator and Overseer of every spirit,
who multiplies the nations on earth.
We beseech You, Lord and Master,
to be our help and provider.
Save those among us who are in trouble,
have mercy on the lowly,
lift up the fallen,
show Yourself to the needy,
heal the ungodly,
convert the wanderers of Your people,
feed the hungry,
release our prisoners,
raise up the weak,
comfort the fainthearted.
Let all the Gentiles know that You are the God alone,
and Jesus Christ is Your Son,
and we are Your people and the sheep of Your pasture.
Yes, Lord, make Your face to shine on us in peace for our good,
that we may be sheltered by Your mighty hand
and delivered from every sin by Your uplifted arm.
And deliver us from those who hate us wrongfully.

O Lord, You alone are able to do these things
and things far better than these for us.
We praise You through the High priest and Guardian of our souls,
Jesus Christ,
through whom be the glory and the majesty
to You both now and for all generations
and for ever and ever.
Amen.

—Clement of Rome (edited)

Christian tradition holds this as the oldest written prayer known outside Scripture.

PRAYER TOOL

RESOURCING PRAYER

Is prayer a line item in your budget for your home, your small group, your business, your organization? Whether it is as simple as buying books on prayer for others (we have a suggested list at www.leadwithprayer.com), food to host a prayer meeting, or making major investments in prayer rooms, prayer coordinators, or prayer events, God invites praying leaders to invest in multiplying prayer.

Some of the ways leaders invested in prayer are:

Physical Space

Whether it's dedicated buildings, dedicated rooms, or renovated multi-purpose rooms, leaders dedicated space in their offices, homes, churches, and buildings to prayer.

Some ministries created 24/7 prayer rooms; others created rooms that are available to their employees, congregations, or even the community.

People

Leaders invested in dedicated prayer roles in their organization in two ways. First was a prayer coordinator who was able to coordinate prayer coverage, disseminate prayer requests around the organization, get volunteer staff for a prayer room, and spend extra time praying.

Second is to pay intercessors to pray part-time for the organization. Some may have misgivings about paying someone to pray, but we pay worship leaders to worship and preachers to study Scripture. Paying someone while they engage in spiritual disciplines like prayer and worship is a tradition that dates back to the book of Leviticus.

Systems

To gather and share prayer requests, ministries often create spreadsheets or databases of prayer requests, along with email lists of intercessors.

To streamline this process for churches, ministries, and companies, we have partnered with the Echo Prayer app to create a beautiful tool to help your organization gather, filter, and share prayer points. Imagine submitting a request and getting an update the next day confirming "three people have prayed for you." Imagine the intercessors in your community receiving timely, specific prayer points to focus their prayers. Check out www.leadwithprayer.com to join us in using this tool.

Schedules

Allowing your employees to pray "on company time" is a real, quantifiable investment that many organizations, both for-profit and nonprofit, have made. Whether it's allowing prayer meetings, quarterly days of prayer, or daily prayer times, this is a tangible way to communicate the value of prayer in any team or organization you lead.

FROM PRAYING LEADER TO BUILDING
A CULTURE OF PRAYER

One Thursday afternoon in 2009, David Denmark, executive director of the Maclellan Foundation, one of the largest and most respected Christian foundations in the United States, hobbled into the hospital for an MRI. Each step was slow and agonizing, as every step had been since he had sustained a back injury earlier in the week. Surgery seemed unavoidable, but with no one available to read the MRI that afternoon, David was sent home to rest and await a follow-up visit with a surgeon, scheduled for the next Tuesday.

Instead of heading home, David drove forty-five minutes out of his way to see a pastor friend with a passion for intercessory prayer. The pastor prayed for David, and although David felt no special sensation or instant healing, in the days that followed, he noticed gradual, continual improvement. By Sunday, he was back on a four-wheeler doing maintenance on his property.

When David returned to the hospital on Tuesday for his follow up visit, he no longer anticipated surgery, but neither did he anticipate the surgeon's reaction upon entering the room. The doctor looked flabbergasted. "Mr. Denmark," he said, "there is no medical reason why you should be feeling your feet, much less standing on them." He shared the MRI results, showing complete impingement of the sciatic nerve. The surgeon had fully expected to see a man who was functionally paralyzed.

As David's body miraculously continued to heal over the coming weeks, he became curious about and captivated by intercessory prayer. If prayer had become this real in his personal life, how could he (and should he) incorporate prayer much more actively into his role as executive director of a grant-making foundation? David shared a plan with his leadership team that would unleash prayer across America to transform the nation—and his team enthusiastically agreed. He had their backing and a $1 million budget to bring this vision to life.

Soon David had assembled the CEOs of major American prayer ministries, orchestrated a unified strategy, built a world-class website, produced a compelling vision-casting video, and distributed numerous seed grants to organizations across the country. Despite these strategies and a lot of compelling "activity," the efforts stalled after months of work. Wanting to kindle a wildfire, they barely lit a spark.

You Cannot Multiply Zero

As David prepared to account to Maclellan's board for the less-than-fruitful investment, he asked God earnestly, "Why didn't this work? I know prayer is important to You, and the country needs it so badly!" In that moment, God convicted David, telling him that he was "multiplying by zero." David's efforts to replicate prayer across the nation were doomed to fail because he was not yet a *person* of prayer. He felt that the Spirit was instructing, "You can't replicate what you do not possess." As conviction brought clarity into his heart, David saw the path forward.

David began to pray quietly in his office, on his knees, alone every morning. No fanfare. No big-name CEOs. No agenda. Just a son talking to his Father and listening for His words of instruction, love, and wisdom. David learned that a healthy culture of prayer starts with a leader who prioritizes praying over strategic programming.

After months of personal prayer, David felt a prompting in his spirit to pray with *others* at Maclellan and model a culture of prayer for the team.

Corporately, the Maclellan Foundation had always valued prayer. For years, they'd started the workweek with all-staff prayer on Mondays. It was already part of the rhythm and routine; however, it often felt more like fulfilling a duty than strategically engaging in a spiritual battle. The dedicated time in prayer was a foundation, but David wanted to build upon that foundation by creating additional space for, and intentionality around, prayer in the organization's life.

His first step was to schedule an additional weekly prayer gathering to exclusively focus on Maclellan's ministry partners. Previously, Monday meeting prayer requests ranged from visionary pleas for revival in a given nation to a staff member's aunt's foot surgery. Both matter! But David decided to make the prayer time more focused. Now the team prays for its ministry partners (grantees) on Mondays and has added a second corporate prayer time on Thursdays to address personal and familial requests.

Internally, as prayer took root in its office culture, the Foundation started talking about "Mission Mondays" and "Family Thursdays." The decision to increase the intentionality during prayer time was a turning point in developing a healthier culture of prayer.

As the Foundation continued in the discipline of prayer and spent time studying what Scripture teaches about prayer, the team came to an important realization: Prayer is not just a means to a spiritual end; it is an end in itself. We may pray to receive things from God, but we also pray to receive God. David explains, "Prayer is not just an input; it's also an outcome."

After months of this "twice a week" rhythm of prayer, David remembered an aphorism from business school: "To see what an organization values, watch where it applies resources."

After seeking the Lord for direction, Maclellan identified thirteen local intercessors who agreed to pray for the Foundation and its ministry partners. David sent these thirteen "Maclellan Intercessors" specific prayer requests each week. During this time, he also learned the importance of reporting results of previous prayers. Semiannually, David gathered the Maclellan Intercessors to build unity, relationships, and momentum. Intercessors even came onsite for board meetings or other strategic events, inviting God's presence, leading, and intervention.

As the prayer initiative grew, tracking both requests and responses became increasingly time-consuming. Not only that, but as David saw results that he could only attribute to prayer, he became increasingly convinced that Maclellan was engaged in a spiritual battle (Ephesians 6:12). "Few of us have the focus and the sense of urgency about prayer that one would expect to see in a life-or-death struggle," he says. "Our opponent in this war is a hundred percent spirit and therefore is not distracted by the things in the natural world. Our enemy can devote a hundred percent of their time to fighting the fight. We will never be able to match that; therefore, we must become very strategic in the struggle. As a result, we determined to become more intentional about prayer."

For David, this meant that prayer deserved someone's dedicated time and attention. He designated a member of the team as Maclellan's part-time prayer coordinator. "Assigning a person to focus on cultivating a culture of prayer was pivotal to our success," recalls David.

Invest in What Matters

An office was remodeled into a prayer room, and one part-time prayer coordinator expanded to three full-time intercessors. As the investment grew, some began to question, why pay people to pray? David felt convicted that this was right, but it was hard to express why until he read in 1 Chronicles of King David's approach to staffing the tabernacle. It says that David employed 288 skilled musicians to make music to the Lord. 1 Chronicles 9:33 reports that these musicians "stayed in the rooms of the temple and were exempt from other duties." King David didn't pay for their talent; he simply bought their time so they were freed from other duties. They, in turn, used their God-given talent to advance the mission of the entity.

Just as the foundation's comptroller was paid to use his talents to provide direction to the Maclellan Foundation, the on-staff intercessors would use their committed time and God-given talent to advance the mission. "We pay for things we think are important," he says. "We have simply elevated prayer to the level of bookkeeping."

In hiring paid intercessors, David wanted to be careful to avoid the temptation of leaving prayer to "the professionals." The prayer room at

Maclellan is, by design, occupied by Maclellan staff of various departments for the first and last fifteen minutes of each day. In between, it is staffed by paid intercessors. "We expect everyone at Maclellan to pray some of the time and someone at Maclellan to be praying all of the time," David says.

Now, when visiting ministry leaders come to Maclellan, they look forward to time in the prayer room. Numerous ministry partners have expressed appreciation for Maclellan's funding partnership yet conveyed a still greater appreciation for the time spent in the prayer room. Local partners schedule time to come to Maclellan's office and pray with Maclellan's intercessory team, and distant ministry partners can pray with the intercessors via Zoom.

CONCLUSION

If we had to sum up Jesus' major teachings and stories on prayer, the overarching theme would be perseverance.

- Ask, seek, knock (Matthew 7:7).
- Always pray and never give up (Luke 18:1).
- "Watch and pray" (Matthew 26:41).
- This kind can only come out through prayer and fasting (Matthew 17:21 NKJV).
- Come to the judge every day until your persistence pays off (Luke 18:6–8).

So many of our interviewees shared incredible stories that demonstrated the power of persistent prayer. Healings. Breakthroughs. Miracles.

But it's possible to miss the hours, days, and years in between. The prayers that did not receive an immediate answer—and the tenacious commitment to *keep praying*. In one particularly moving conversation, a friend shared with us not only about a miraculous answer to prayer but also about the discouragement she experienced during the decade-long battle that preceded it. She felt called to pray an hour each Sunday for her family members who did not know Jesus. They had all endured abuse, and when she began praying, every single one of them was addicted to drugs or alcohol.

By year seven of praying for her family an hour every week, nothing had happened. Years eight and nine were just the same. Hanging on in persistent prayer seemed to get harder with each passing day and year. But in year ten, every single one of her family members, in different ways, became passionate followers of Christ. Their lives have been radically transformed.

We never know where we are in the story, and not every story ends in physical healing, financial provision, or relational restoration on this side of heaven. Yet even in these painful moments of seemingly unanswered prayer, we still believe that it's worth it.

Grit and tenacity are prerequisites for leadership, and if we are to lead with prayer, then Christ invites and invokes us to bring these same attributes to our prayer life—to *keep praying*.

We affirm with Gary Haugen that "prayer matters." We believe with Joni Eareckson Tada that prayer is not about just changed circumstances but changed selves. And we know from personal experience that it's possible to encounter God when we're on our knees with our face pressed to the carpet.

Sometimes the answer to our prayers is a *miracle*; other times it is a *moment* in His presence. In the final analysis, perhaps this is the greatest miracle of all. Either way, the miraculous comes through persistent prayer.

A common leadership axiom says, "The definition of insanity is doing the same thing and expecting different results." By this definition, persistent prayer is insane.

But so is cutting down a tree: swinging an ax again and again with the expectation that the tree will eventually fall. If one feels crazier than the other, that's only because the results of swinging an ax are visible, while outcomes achieved in prayer are often not. Even when we see no results, God commands us to pray persistently, chipping away at the fallen world, chipping away at our own stubborn self-sufficiency, and ushering in a new Kingdom in our lives, our leadership, and beyond as we "fix our eyes not on what is seen, but on what is unseen, since what is seen is temporary, but what is unseen is eternal" (2 Corinthians 4:18).

A Final Word

As leaders—but more fundamentally as Jesus' followers—we persevere in prayer, and our prayers persevere beyond us. Scripture teaches that we may not see the fruition of our prayers in our lifetime, but it also gives us hope that our prayers can live on past our lifetime (Hebrews 11:39).

I (Ryan) learned to pray and developed a passion for prayer from my mother. I can remember my mom praying late into the night, night after night, when I was a young boy. From her prayer room, she would cry out to God for us, for our neighborhood, and for the nations. I will never forget staying up late, listening with my ear to the door to hear my mom's prayers. The desperate prayers of my mother before God ring in my ears to this day.

She told me something she felt the Lord had spoken to her in one of those evening prayer times: "There are prayers I'm still working on that you forgot you prayed many years ago."

God never forgets a prayer. Even generations later.

In one of our last interviews, Mark Batterson talked about his grandfather's legacy of prayer.

Mark shared how his own life of service and church leadership is fulfilling many of his grandfather's prayers, even though his grandfather passed away decades ago. The prayers of his grandfather lived on and are being answered in his life.

We have the power to pray prayers into the future—prayers to be answered generations from now. Prayer can be not only present hope but also the foundation of future blessing.

Jesus practiced this type of generational prayer in the Garden, late at night, just before His arrest, torture, and death. His mind and heart journeyed past the cross into the future as He prayed not just for His disciples. "My prayer is not for them alone. I pray also for those who will believe in me through their message," He said (John 17:20). Jesus' prayer is crossing through time even to our generation, even to us.

A friend shared a story of a beautifully redemptive mission trip to Russia after the fall of communism that poignantly illustrates this concept.

The team was commissioned to take the stones of a former Russian gulag, a forced labor camp where prisoners endured horrific conditions, and use those stones to construct the foundation of a new church building.

Despite the hard work, the team was captivated by the poetic picture of repurposing the stones that built a place of despair to become the foundation of a house of worship. Several days into the deconstruction process, a team member found a canister amid the rubble of the gulag. There was a note inside.

The team took the note to their hosting pastor, and he cried as he read the words:

> *We are a community of believers being forced to take the stones of our church and use them to build our own prison. We pray one day God will hear us and use these stones to build a church again.*

Every prayer we pray is like hiding a canister in the rubble of this world. Prayers that a loving Father has promised not to forget.

As we pray for our families, organizations, staff, and those we seek to reach with our ministries, we can slip our prayers into canisters for future generations. And as we train others to pray, their prayers, too, will go on for generations—until we see the culmination of all our hopes, prayers, and dreams in the face of Jesus.

Come, Lord Jesus.

PRAYER

Jesus,
Teach me to pray.
Help me awaken the dawn with praise and thanksgiving.
Help me abide in You in the moments of each day.
Help me welcome the evening with grateful worship.
Help me watch and pray with You into the night.
Show me the joy of Your presence in the trials I face.
Show me Your miraculous power in my neighborhood and in the
*   nations.*
Show me Your wisdom in the secret place.
Show me the freedom of Your forgiveness.
Teach me to fight on my knees against the forces of darkness.
Teach me to listen to Your whispers in the noise of this world.
Teach me to rely on Your strength when the world weighs on me.
Teach me to cast my cares on You when anxieties rise.
Teach me to surrender when my heart wants to stray.
May I learn to fall on my knees in humility.
May I learn to rise up in resurrection power.
In dark nights, may I hold fast to Your love.
In bright days, may I not forget Your blessings.
Then my soul will walk with You in the garden in the cool of the day.
Teach me to pray, Lord.
Teach me to pray.

—Ryan Skoog

CHECKLIST FOR BECOMING
A PRAYING LEADER

Practice	Prayer Tool
____ Create space for friendship	Walk with God guide (page 19)
____ Create a plan, a Rule of Life, around prayer	Prayer map (page 36)
____ Create prompts to remember Jesus throughout the day	One-sentence prayers (page 51)
____ Practice posture	Engaging posture in prayer (page 63)
____ Pray through tough times	Psalms to pray during tough times (page 79)
____ Pray Scripture	*Lectio Divina* (page 90)
____ Learn to listen	Steps to hearing God (page 107)
____ Humbly repent	*Examen* (page 117)
____ Create a fasting schedule	Guide to fasting for leaders (page 128)
____ Create a retreat schedule	Richard Beaumont's guide to an effective personal retreat (page 138)
____ Build a culture of prayer	Steps toward a culture of prayer (page 155)
____ Pray for those you lead	Pray your org chart (page 169)
____ Have a team of prayer partners	Steps to building personal prayer teams (page 180)
____ Invest in prayer	Resourcing prayer (page 196)

ACKNOWLEDGMENTS

In the introduction, we acknowledged that this book was "written in community." It's our privilege to express gratitude to a few members of that community whose contributions shaped our thinking and writing.

There is one person whose tireless passion and incredible gifts wove together the words of three different writers and crafted them into a book. Without her, this book would never have happened. Jill Heisey, thank you.

Andrew Wolgemuth, our literary agent, is as kind as he is wise. He was an expert guide throughout the entire book-writing process.

To the team at Hachette and FaithWords, particularly Ryan Peterson, who first believed in this book and whose clarifying edits significantly improved the manuscript, we are grateful. We prayed for the right publisher, and those prayers were answered in you.

To all the praying leaders, past and present, thank you for your example of what it looks like to lead with prayer. You inspire us. To those who allowed us to sit at your feet and learn from you, we lead differently as a result. Thank you.

We could (and should!) say more about each of these very special family members and friends who supported us throughout this book-writing process. We are truly blessed to have amazing colleagues, supportive friends, and devoted families.

Ryan: Rach, Colones, Syd-the-Kid, Jay Dizzle, Captain, Ma'am, Bishop, A-aron, Amigo, Princeton, Furina, Si, Mr. Oo, Bear, Bahinī, London Al, Rico, Brad, Jerry, Rob, Madam Pres, Brent, Micah, Leak, Fred, Kee, Kuku, Ganesh, and Rosebell.

Peter: Laurel, Keith, Liliana, Myles, London, Baxter (executive producer), Megan, LeAnna, Brianna, Claire, Jeff, Joshua, Alaina, Christine, Judah, Dan, Isabel, Pierson, Ashley, Phil, Greg, the commissioner, the HOPE board, Lance, Bill, and Ryan and Abi from Paulding Fair.

Cameron: Carolyn, Grace, Christiana, Hewson, Sandhana, Catherine, Keziah, Abi, Emanuel, Grace, John Mark, David, David, David, David, Sam, Travis, and Tyler.

Ultimately, thank You, Jesus. All from You. All through You. All for You.

NOTES

Introduction

1. This story was shared by Billy Graham's grandson, Stephan Tchividjian, who remembers his grandfather as a man of prayer who was often on his face in humility before God, confessing that he could not speak unless God touched him with grace. Stephan Tchividjian, interview by Ryan Skoog, February 24, 2023.

2. "Most Pastors Unsatisfied with Their Personal Prayer Lives," *Baptist Press*, June 6, 2005, https://www.baptistpress.com/resource-library/news/most-pastors-unsatisfied-with-their-personal-prayer-lives/.

3. "The Greatest Needs of Pastors," *Lifeway Research*, March–April 2021, https://research.lifeway.com/wp-content/uploads/2022/01/The-Greatest-Needs-of-Pastors-Phase-2-Quantitative-Report-Release-1.pdf.

4. The foundation that commissioned the study wished to remain anonymous but granted members of our team the opportunity to review the study's findings on the condition of anonymity.

5. Tim Keller, "New York City Gathering NYC 2018: The Primacy of Prayer," *New City Network*, June 7, 2018, video, https://www.youtube.com/watch?v=KeKWjd4fe5E&t=44s.

6. Tim Keller, "Bonus Episode: A Conversation with Tim Keller," interview by Mike Cosper, *The Rise and Fall of Mars Hill*, July 1, 2022, podcast, 1:02:14, https://www.christianitytoday.com/ct/podcasts/rise-and-fall-of-mars-hill/tim-keller-mike-cosper-mars-hill-bonus.html.

7. J. Robert Clinton, "Listen Up Leaders!" Barnabas Publishers (1989): 18, https://clintonleadership.com/resources/complimentary/ListenUpLeaders.pdf. Clinton conducted his study in the early 1990s. Not all the leaders Clinton identified were described in enough detail to be evaluated, but of those who were, only about 30 percent finished well by Clinton's definition: "walking with God in a vibrant personal relationship, developing the potential God has given to its appropriate capacity, and leaving behind an ultimate contribution that is both pleasing to God and established by Him." Clinton applied this same standard to more than 1,200 historical and contemporary leaders and reached an equally startling conclusion: "Evidence from today indicates that this ratio is probably generous. Probably less than one in three are finishing well today." See J. Robert Clinton, *The Making of a Leader*, 2nd ed. (Colorado Springs: NavPress, 2012).

8. J. Robert Clinton, *The Making of a Leader*, 2nd ed. (Colorado Springs: NavPress, 2012), 210.

9. "Status of Global Christianity, 2022, in the Context of 1900–2050," *Center for the Study of Global Christianity at Gordon-Conwell Theological Seminary*, accessed March 6, 2023, https://www.gordonconwell.edu/center-for-global-christianity/wp-content /uploads/sites/13/2022/01/Status-of-Global-Christianity-2022.pdf; Aaron Earls, "Ten Encouraging Trends in Global Christianity in 2020," *Lifeway Research*, June 10, 2020, https://research.lifeway.com/2020/06/10/10-encouraging-trends-of-global-christianity -in-2020/; Y Bonesteele, "How the Growing Global Church Can Encourage American Christians," *Lifeway Research*, March 17, 2021, https://research.lifeway.com/2021/03 /17/how-the-growing-global-church-can-encourage-american-christians/.

10. For the security of our interviewees and their ongoing ministries, we have deferred to their preferences in using only first names or pseudonyms and withholding precise locations.

11. David Watson and Paul Watson, *Contagious Disciple Making: Leading Others on a Journey of Discovery* (Nashville: Thomas Nelson, 2014); Ying Kai and Grace Kai, *Ying & Grace Kai's Training For Trainers: The Movement That Changed the World* (Monument, CO: Wigtake Resources LLC, 2018). See also the works of researcher David Garrison.

12. Justin Taylor, "George Verwer's Conversion: 60 Years Ago Today God Created a Global Evangelist," *The Gospel Coalition*, March 3, 2015, https://www.thegospel coalition.org/blogs/justin-taylor/george-verwers-conversion-60-years-ago-today -god-created-a-global-evangelist/.

13. "History," *Operation Mobilization USA*, accessed March 6, 2023, https://www.omusa .org/about/history/.

14. "Silent and Solo: How Americans Pray," *Barna Group*, August 15, 2017, https:// www.barna.com/research/silent-solo-americans-pray/.

15. Stephen Macchia, *Crafting a Rule of Life: An Invitation to the Well-Ordered Way* (Downers Grove, IL: InterVarsity Press, 2012), 29.

16. Christian Dawson, "Ephesians: Immeasurably More: Part 10: Stand," *Bridgetown Audio Podcast*, September 4, 2022, bridgetown.podbean.com/e/part-10-stand/.

17. "Be Thou My Vision," translation of Irish hymn "Bí Thusa 'mo Shúile," translated into English in 1905.

Chapter 1

1. "Prayer in Christian Organizations," *Barna Group*, 2020.

2. Rosebell, interview by Ryan Skoog, February 11, 2019. For her safety, we cannot identify Rosebell's location or surname.

3. Oswald Chambers, "Are You Fresh for Everything?" *My Utmost for His Highest*, accessed September 11, 2023, https://utmost.org/are-you-fresh-for-everything/.

4. John Kim, interview by Ryan Skoog, December 7, 2021.

5. Ibrahim Omondi, interview by Peter Greer, February 3, 2023.

6. C. S. Lewis, *Letters to Malcolm: Chiefly on Prayer* (San Francisco: HarperOne, 2017), 125.

7. G. K. Chesterton, *Orthodoxy* (London: John Lane Company, 1909), 298.

8. Gerard Manley Hopkins, "As Kingfishers Catch Fire," accessed March 6, 2023, https://www.poetryfoundation.org/poems/44389/as-kingfishers-catch -fire.

9. Jacob Hess, "Celebrating the Relentless Love of God: A Conversation with the Beloved Rev. Francis Chan," *Deseret News*, December 5, 2021, https://www.deseret .com/2021/12/4/22796535/celebrating-the-relentless-love-of-god-a-conversation -with-the-rev-francis-chan-evangelical-lds.

10. Quotes in this section not otherwise attributed are from Francis Chan, interview by Cameron Doolittle, February 19, 2023.

11. Francis Chan, "Prayer Makes a Leader," BRMinistries, 2:33 and 5:13, November 30, 2018, video, https://www.youtube.com/watch?v=y9AUr6xic2Q&t=327s&ab _channel=BRMinistries.

12. Hess, "Celebrating the Relentless Love of God."

13. Henri Nouwen, *Beloved: Henri Nouwen in Conversation* (Norwich, UK: Canterbury Press, 2007), 30–31.

14. Mother Teresa interview with Dan Rather, as quoted in Ron Mehl, *What God Whispers in the Night* (Sisters, Oregon: Multnomah, 2000), 97.

15. St. Teresa of Kolkata, *Everything Starts from Prayer* (Ashland, OR: White Cloud Press, 2018), 1.

16. Summer Allen, "The Science of Awe," Greater Good Science Center at UC Berkeley, September 2018, https://ggsc.berkeley.edu/images/uploads/GGSC-JTF_White _Paper-Awe_FINAL.pdf.

17. Charles Austin Miles, "In the Garden," 1912.

Chapter 2

1. Marjorie J. Thompson, *Soul Feast: An Invitation to the Christian Spiritual Life* (Louisville, KY: Westminster John Knox, 2014), 150.

2. John Piper, "If You Don't Pray, You Won't Live," Desiring God, October 31, 2018, https://www.desiringgod.org/messages/put-in-the-fire-for-the-sake-of-prayer /excerpts/if-you-dont-pray-you-wont-live.

3. John Mark Comer, "Prayer Part 9: Fixed Hour Prayer," *Bridgetown Church*, July 3, 2017, https://vimeo.com/224118521.

4. As quoted in John Ortberg, *Soul Keeping: Caring for the Most Important Part of You* (Grand Rapids, MI: Zondervan, 2014), 89.

5. Comer, "Prayer Part 9: Fixed Hour Prayer."

6. Daniel Kahneman, *Thinking, Fast and Slow* (New York: Farrar, Straus and Giroux, 2011).

7. Barbara Bradley Hagerty, "Prayer May Reshape Your Brain...and Your Reality," *NPR*, May 20, 2009, https://www.npr.org/2009/05/20/104310443/prayer-may -reshape-your-brain-and-your-reality.

8. Andrew Newberg, "How Do Meditation and Prayer Change Our Brains?" accessed March 7, 2023, http://www.andrewnewberg.com/research.

9. For more on Newberg's research, see http://www.andrewnewberg.com/research, as well as Andrew Newberg and Mark Robert Waldman, *How God Changes Your Brain: Breakthrough Findings from a Leading Neuroscientist* (New York: Ballantine Books, 2009), 23–27. Newberg's book mentions a study on how Buddhist meditation changes the brain. Later, Newberg repeated a similar test with praying nuns that evidenced increased activity in the inferior parietal lobe as well as the frontal lobes. Newberg's research was accessed online April 5, 2023.

10. Peter Boelens, Roy Reeves, William Replogle, Harold Koenig, "A Randomized Trial of the Effect of Prayer on Depression and Anxiety," *International Journal of Psychiatry in Medicine* 39, no. 4 (2009): 377–92, https://doi.org/10.2190/PM.39.4.c.

11. Andrew Newberg, interview by Michael Sandler, "How God Changes the Brain! Neuroscience of Prayer, Spirituality and Meditation!" *Michael Sandler's Inspire Nation*, July 28, 2020, https://www.youtube.com/watch?v=qp_sqMIOMcs&ab_channel=MichaelSandler%27sInspireNation.

12. Hagerty, "Prayer May Reshape Your Brain . . . and Your Reality."

13. Newberg, interview by Michael Sandler.

14. Amy Wachholtz and Kenneth Pargament, "Is Spirituality a Critical Ingredient of Meditation? Comparing the Effects of Spiritual Meditation, Secular Meditation, and Relaxation on Spiritual, Psychological, Cardiac, and Pain Outcomes," *Journal of Behavioral Medicine* 28, no. 4 (August 2005): 369-384, https://doi.org/10.1007/s10865-005-9008-5.

15. Christine Larson, "Health Prayer: Should Religion and Faith Have Roles in Medicine?" *U.S. News & World Report*, December 22, 2008, https://health.usnews.com/health-news/articles/2008/12/22/health-prayer-should-religion-and-faith-have-roles-in-medicine.

16. Shalom is a pseudonym, used to protect our interviewee and his ministry.

Chapter 3

1. Brother Lawrence, *The Practice of the Presence of God: The Best Rule of Holy Life* (Grand Rapids: Christian Classics Ethereal Library, 1994), https://ccel.org/ccel/l/lawrence/practice/cache/practice.pdf. Lawrence's book *The Practice of the Presence of God* has sold more than 20 million copies.

2. Henri J. M. Nouwen, foreword to *The Practice of the Presence of God*, trans. John Delaney (New York: Image, 1977), 10.

3. "Loves, Hobby Lobby Recognized among Forbes Largest Private Companies List," *News 9*, November 9, 2010, https://www.news9.com/story/5e35b38e83eff40362bee303/loves-hobby-lobby-recognized-among-forbes-largest-private-companies-list.

4. David Green, personal communication with Ryan Skoog, February 3, 2018.

5. David Green, *Giving It All Away . . . and Getting It All Back Again: The Way of Living Generously* (Grand Rapids, MI: Zondervan, 2017).

6. David Green, "The Importance of Family Legacy with David Green Pt. 1," interview by Ray Hilbert, *Truth at Work*, September 25, 2018, podcast, 7:22, https://truthatwork.org/the-importance-of-family-legacy-with-david-green-pt-1/.

7. Green, *Giving It All Away*.

8. "God be in my head," *The Oxford Book of Prayer*, ed. Appleton, © 1985, 1992.

9. J. D. Watson, *A Word for the Day: Key Words from the New Testament* (Chattanooga, TN: AMG Publishers, 2006).

10. Dallas Willard, *The Great Omission: Reclaiming Jesus's Essential Teachings on Discipleship* (San Francisco: HarperCollins, 2006), 125.

11. Zehra is a pseudonym, used to protect our interviewee and her ministry.

12. Zehra, interview by Cameron Doolittle, January 26, 2023.

13. Dolores Smyth, "What Is the Origin and Purpose of Church Bells?" Christianity.com, July 16, 2019, https://www.christianity.com/wiki/church/what-is-the-origin-and-purpose-of-church-bells.html.

14. Mark Zhou, interview by Cameron Doolittle, November 10, 2021.

15. HELPS Word-studies, s.v. "Proseuchomai," accessed March 16, 2023, https://biblehub.com/greek/4336.htm.

16. Brother Lawrence, *The Practice of the Presence of God*.

17. In the book *Words Can Change Your Brain*, Andrew Newberg, a neuroscientist at Thomas Jefferson University, and Mark Robert Waldman, a communications expert, state, "a single word has the power to influence the expression of genes that regulate physical and emotional stress."

Chapter 4

1. Justin Whitmel Earley, interview by Peter Greer, January 6, 2023.

2. Justin Whitmel Earley, *The Common Rule: Habits of Purpose for an Age of Distraction* (Grand Rapids, MI: InterVarsity Press, 2019), 37.

3. Earley interview.

4. Eusebius Pamphilus, *The Ecclesiastical History of Eusebius Pamphilus: Bishop of Cesarea, in Palestine*, trans. Christian Frederick Crusé (New York: T. N. Stanford, 1856), 76.

5. Edward Bounds, *E. M. Bounds on Prayer* (Peabody: Hendrickson Publishers, 2006), 6.

6. Pope Emeritus Benedict XVI, "The Theology of Kneeling," *Adoremus*, November 15, 2022, https://adoremus.org/2002/11/the-theology-of-kneeling/.

7. John Ortberg, interview by Cameron Doolittle, March 13, 2023.

8. Don Millican, interview by Peter Greer, January 18, 2023.

9. Kathryn Reid, "1994 Rwandan Genocide, Aftermath: Facts, FAQs, and How to Help," World Vision, April 1, 2019, https://www.worldvision.org/refugees-news-stories/1994-rwandan-genocide-facts.

10. Christine Baingana, interview by Peter Greer, May 20, 2022.

11. "Angaza Awards 2022 Top Finalist; Christine Baingana," *Kenyan Wall Street*, January 18, 2022, https://kenyanwallstreet.com/angaza-awards-2022-top-finalist-christine-baingana/.

Chapter 5

1. My (Ryan's) brother and business partner was interviewed for this article. Rachel Siegel, "Congress Needs to Weigh In on Expanding Main Street Loan Program to

More Businesses, Boston Fed Chief Says," *Washington Post*, September 8, 2020, https://www.washingtonpost.com/business/2020/09/08/main-street-fed-loans.

2. C. S. Lewis, *Till We Have Faces* (San Francisco: HarperOne, 2017), 269.

3. Joni Eareckson Tada, *Seeking God: My Journey of Prayer and Praise Reflections* (Brentwood, TN: Wolgemuth & Hyatt, 1991).

4. Joni Eareckson Tada, "Heartfelt, Honest Prayers," *Joni and Friends*, January 2, 2022, https://www.joniandfriends.org/heartfelt-honest-prayers/.

5. Joni Eareckson Tada, interview by Peter Greer, February 2, 2023.

6. "Joni Eareckson Tada Shares Her Story," *Joni and Friends*, January 28, 2014, video, 6:45, https://www.youtube.com/watch?v=VVXJ8GyLgt0.

7. Tom Fowler, "No. 1 Private Company: Texon," *Houston Chronicle*, June 6, 2011, https://www.chron.com/business/article/No-1-private-company-Texon-1683065.php.

8. Terry Looper, *Sacred Pace: Four Steps to Hearing God and Aligning Yourself with His Will* (Nashville: Thomas Nelson, 2019).

9. Terry Looper, interview by Ryan Skoog, July 25, 2022.

10. Ganesh is a pseudonym, used to protect our interviewee.

11. Ganesh, interview by Ryan Skoog, July 26, 2022.

12. Mike Cosper, "Bonus Episode: Paint the Beauty We Split: A Conversation with Chad Gardner," *The Rise and Fall of Mars Hill*, May 5, 2022, podcast, https://www.christianitytoday.com/ct/podcasts/rise-and-fall-of-mars-hill/mars-hill-podcast-chad-gardner-kings-kaleidoscope.html.

13. Helen H. Lemmel, "Turn Your Eyes upon Jesus," 1922.

Chapter 6

1. Tim Mackie, email message to Cameron Doolittle, May 2023.

2. Tim Mackie, "Paradise Now," *24-7 Prayer USA*, October 12, 2022, video, https://www.youtube.com/watch?v=HQlH-WfmZms&t=735s.

3. Tim Mackie, interview by Cameron Doolittle, April 21, 2020.

4. Ibid.

5. Tim Mackie, "Paradise Now."

6. Japhet Yanmekaa, email message to Cameron Doolittle, February 17, 2023.

7. Japhet Yanmekaa, interview by Cameron Doolittle, December 11, 2020.

8. While not all of these were prayers, Shari Abbott has compiled a list of times Jesus quoted from Psalms, His prayer book. Access the full list at https://reasonsforhopejesus.com/old-testament-book-jesus-quote-often/.

9. Alexander McLean, "Justice Defenders *Lectio Divina*" (introduction, Zoom meeting, January 26, 2023).

10. Alexander McLean, interview by Peter Greer, July 2, 2021.

11. John Piper, "How Do I Pray the Bible?" *Desiring God: Ask Pastor John*, February 6, 2017, podcast, 0:45, https://www.desiringgod.org/interviews/how-do-i-pray-the-bible.

12. John Piper, "How to Pray for Half-an-Hour," *Desiring God*, January 5, 1982, https://www.desiringgod.org/articles/how-to-pray-for-half-an-hour.

13. John Piper, "Should I Use the Bible When I Pray?" *Desiring God*, September 28, 2007, https://www.desiringgod.org/interviews/should-i-use-the-bible-when-i-pray.
14. Piper, "Should I Use the Bible When I Pray?"
15. Piper, "How to Pray for Half-an-Hour."
16. John Piper, "Learning to Pray in the Spirit and the Word, Part 1," *Desiring God*, December 31, 2000, https://www.desiringgod.org/messages/learning-to-pray-in-the-spirit-and-the-word-part-1.
17. We quote liberally, and with permission, from https://www.soulshepherding.org/lectio-divina-guides/.
18. Henri Nouwen, *Spiritual Direction: Wisdom for the Long Walk of Faith* (New York: Harper Collins, 2006), xvii–xviii.
19. Courtesy of Bill Gaultiere and Soul Shepherding.

Chapter 7

1. Brother Andrew, *God's Smuggler*, ex. ed. (Minneapolis: Chosen, 2015), 60.
2. Timothy D. Wilson, et al., "Just Think: The Challenges of the Disengaged Mind," *Science*, July 1, 2014.
3. Terry Looper, interview by Ryan Skoog, July 25, 2022.
4. Aila Tasse, interview by Cameron Doolittle, August 25, 2022.
5. Aila Tasse, WhatsApp message to Cameron Doolittle, February 16, 2023.
6. Tasse interview.
7. Priscilla Shirer, "Learn How to Recognize God's Voice," *Praise on TBN*, March 3, 2022, https://www.youtube.com/watch?v=iyBQXFYQ3P0.
8. Philip Yancey, "Where the Light Fell," interview by Dave and Ann Wilson, *Family Life Today*, February 16, 2023, podcast, https://www.truthnetwork.com/show/family-life-today-dave-ann-wilson-bob-lepine/56629/.
9. John English, *Spiritual Intimacy and Community: An Ignatian View of the Small Faith Community* (Mahwah, NJ: Paulist Press: 1993).
10. George Müller, *Answers to Prayer*, accessed April 5, 2023, http://storage.cloversites.com/mountainview/documents/Answers%20To%20Prayer%20by%20George%20Mueller.pdf, 2–3.

Chapter 8

1. Jamie Rasmussen, "Unveiled," Scottsdale Bible Church, November 20, 2022, video, 1:05:37, https://scottsdalebible.com/message/?enmse=1&enmse_sid=121&enmse_mid=622.
2. Rob Ketterling, interview by Ryan Skoog, February 6, 2023.
3. Jean is a pseudonym, used to protect our interviewee.
4. George Aschenbrenner, *Consciousness Examen*, accessed December 8, 2022, https://www.ignatianspirituality.com/ignatian-prayer/the-examen/consciousness-examen/.

5. St. Ignatius, *The Spiritual Exercises of St. Ignatius* (New York: Random House, 2000), 20.

6. Rachel Adelman, "The Burning Bush: Why Must Moses Remove His Shoes?" *TheTorah.com*, January 7, 2021, https://www.thetorah.com/article/the-burning-bush -why-must-moses-remove-his-shoes.

7. Ignatius, *The Spiritual Exercises of St. Ignatius*.

Chapter 9

1. Patrick Johnson, interview by Cameron Doolittle, January 24, 2022.

2. Patrick Johnson, email to Cameron Doolittle, March 30, 2023.

3. Japhet Yanmekaa, interview by Cameron Doolittle, December 11, 2020.

4. For the security of our interviewee and his ongoing ministry, we have deferred to his preference in withholding his name and location.

5. Pavel is a pseudonym, used to protect our interviewee and his ministry.

6. Stan Parks, interview by Ryan Skoog, September 23, 2021. Stan leads 24:14, a community committed to seeing church planting movements in every unreached people group and place.

7. Pavel, interview by Ryan Skoog, November 27, 2021.

8. R. Joseph Owles, *The Didache: The Teaching of the Twelve Apostles* (CreateSpace, 2014), 14.

9. St. Basil, as quoted in Kent Berghuis, "Christian Fasting, Appendix 1: Basil's Sermons About Fasting," Bible.org, https://bible.org/seriespage/appendix-1-basil%E2%80%99s -sermons-about-fasting#P1625_606319, accessed April 1, 2023.

10. St. John Chrysostom, as quoted by Sergei Bulgakov, "Fasting according to the Church Fathers," *Orthodox Christianity Then and Now*, https://www.johnsanidopoulos .com/2013/03/fasting-according-to-church-fathers.html, accessed April 1, 2023.

11. St. Isaac the Syrian, as quoted by Sergei Bulgakov, "Fasting according to the Church Fathers," *Orthodox Christianity Then and Now*, https://www.johnsanidopoulos .com/2013/03/fasting-according-to-church-fathers.html, accessed April 1, 2023.

12. Joan Brueggeman Rufe, *Early Christian Fasting: A Study of Creative Adaptation* (Ann Arbor: UMI, 1994), iii.

13. Kent Berghuis, *Christian Fasting: A Theological Approach*, 2007, https://bible.org /book/export/html/6521.

14. Dallas Willard, "Real Lyfe - Dallas Willard - Hooked (Extra: fasting)" *Lyfe videos by Bible Society*, October 11, 2010, 0:38, https://www.youtube.com/watch?v =oocf0eoAy5I&t=37s.

15. Dallas Willard, "Dallas' Personal Daily Practices?" interview by Bobby Schuller, *Tree of Life Community*, August 16, 2011, https://www.youtube.com/watch?v =GqLmeubS65Q.

16. Dallas Willard, *Life without Lack* (Nashville: Nelson Books, 2018), 14.

17. Willard, *Life without Lack*.

18. Yanmekaa interview.

Chapter 10

1. Hala Saad, interview by Cameron Doolittle, January 17, 2022.
2. Richard Foster, *Devotional Classics*, rev. ed. (New York: HarperCollins, 2005), 85.
3. Brian Cavanaugh, *Sower's Seeds of Encouragement: Fifth Planting* (New York: Paulist Press, 1998), 32.
4. Tim Mackie, "Paradise Now," *24-7 Prayer USA*, October 12, 2022, video, https://www.youtube.com/watch?v=HQlH-WfmZms&t=735s.
5. Dallas Willard, *Renovation of the Heart,* 20th anniv. ed. (Colorado Springs: NavPress, 2021), 84.
6. Richard Beaumont, personal email to Cameron Doolittle, September 6, 2022.
7. Evelyn Underhill, *The Ways of the Spirit* (New York: Crossroad, 1994), 50–51.

Chapter 11

1. Mark Batterson, interview by Ryan Skoog, December 20, 2022.
2. Steve Shackelford, interview by Ryan Skoog, January 9, 2023.
3. Steve Shackelford, Redeemer City to City, March 9, 2022, https://facebook.com/RedeemerCTC/videos/449542340289304.
4. "History Is Being Made, Right Now. Be a Part of It," *YouVersion*, May 8, 2017, https://blog.youversion.com/2017/05/history-made-right-now-part/.
5. Todd Peterson, interview by Cameron Doolittle, March 26, 2023.
6. "Who We Are," *Life in Abundance International*, accessed March 23, 2023, https://lifeinabundance.org/who-we-are/.
7. This and the following quotes, unless otherwise noted, are from Florence Muindi, *The Pursuit of His Calling: Following in Purpose* (Nashville: Integrity Publishers Inc., 2008).
8. Florence Muindi, interview by Chris Horst and Jill Heisey, October 19, 2020.
9. Gil Odendaal, interview by Peter Greer, October 26, 2021.
10. Edward Bounds, *E. M. Bounds on Prayer* (Peabody, MA: Hendrickson Publishers, 2006), 165.

Chapter 12

1. David Wills, personal email to Cameron Doolittle, March 13, 2023.
2. David Sykora, interview by Cameron Doolittle, January 13, 2023.
3. Recounted by David Syokra in interview with Cameron Doolittle, January 13, 2023.
4. Christine Caine, "Intercession with Christine Caine," interview by Tyler Staton, *Praying Like Monks, Living Like Fools*, October 31, 2022, https://www.youtube.com/watch?v=eldI4RHxhUY.
5. André Mann, interview by Peter Greer, June 15, 2021.

Chapter 13

1. John Onwuchekwa, *Prayer: How Praying Together Shapes the Church* (Wheaton, IL: Crossway, 2018), 41.

2. "Silent and Solo: How Americans Pray," *Barna Group*, August 17, 2017, https://www.barna.com/research/silent-solo-americans-pray/.
3. Based on review of the first fifty images on September 30, 2022.
4. Peter Kubasek, interview by Cameron Doolittle, January 20, 2021.
5. Judah Mooney, interview by Peter Greer, March 30, 2023.
6. Group prayers in Acts: 1:13–14, 2:42–46, 4:24–31, 8:14–15, 12:5–12, 13:1–3, 14:23, 16:13–16, 20:36, 21:5–6, 27:29.

Chapter 14

1. Leslie Tarr, "A Prayer Meeting That Lasted for 100 Years," *Christian History* 1, no. 1, 1982, https://www.christianitytoday.com/history/issues/issue-1/prayer-meeting-that-lasted-100-years.html.
2. Jay Martin, interview by Peter Greer, June 16, 2021.
3. Mary Elizabeth Ellett, interview by Peter Greer, November 12, 2021.
4. Gary Haugen, "GPG 2015: Prayer Matters—An Introduction," *International Justice Mission*, April 18, 2015, 5:07, https://www.youtube.com/watch?v=_lBwdRuuz8Y.
5. Jim Martin, Vice President of Spiritual Formation at International Justice Mission, interview by Peter Greer, June 30, 2021.
6. Haugen, "GPG 2015: Prayer Matters—An Introduction."

ABOUT THE AUTHORS

Ryan Skoog is a founder of several travel technology companies, including Faith Ventures and Yonder Travel Insurance. He also co-founded and leads the nonprofit VENTURE.ORG, which serves the tough places of the world by partnering with local leaders to plant thousands of churches and empowering these leaders to rescue girls from trafficking, start farms, initiate microenterprises, train in feminine hygiene, and serve war refugees. This leads to generational transformation in some of the unsafe, unreached, unresourced regions of the world. Ryan is the co-author of *Chosen* with Outreach Publishing.

Peter Greer is the president and CEO of HOPE International, a global Christ-centered economic development organization serving throughout Africa, Asia, Latin America, and Eastern Europe. Prior to joining HOPE, Peter worked internationally as a microfinance adviser in Cambodia and Zimbabwe and as managing director for Urwego Bank in Rwanda. Peter has co-authored fifteen books, including *Mission Drift*, which was selected as a Book Award Winner from *Christianity Today*, *Rooting for Rivals*, *The Gift of Disillusionment*, and *The Spiritual Danger of Doing Good*.

Cameron Doolittle is senior advisor to the Maclellan Foundation, executive director of John Mark Comer's Practicing the Way, and co-founder of Generosity Path. He previously served as an advisor to senators, congressmen, and senior executives at Fortune 500 companies through his consulting firm, since acquired by Gartner. Cameron advises influential givers and great ministries. He now consults with organizations that his family loves, including BibleProject, Desiring God, Faith Driven, ECFA, Awana, *Christianity Today*, YoungLife, and others. He served as founding CEO of Jill's House, a ministry for kids with intellectual disabilities.